A FAR JOURNEY

A FAR JOURNEY

BY

ABRAHAM MITRIE RIHBANY

WITH ILLUSTRATIONS

BOSTON AND NEW YORK
HOUGHTON MIFFLIN COMPANY
The Riverside Press Cambridge
1914

Published September 1914

TO MY WIFE

AND TO THE MANY AMERICAN CITIZENS WHO
BY THEIR WISE AND FRIENDLY COUNSEL
LENT ME GUIDANCE AND INSPIRATION IN
SEEKING MY AMERICAN HERITAGE; WHO BY
THEIR LOYALTY TO THE IDEAL REALITIES
DEEPENED MY FAITH IN GOD AND MAN

THIS VOLUME IS GRATEFULLY
DEDICATED

PREFACE

IT may not be uninteresting to the reader to know how this autobiography came to be written, and what the author considers to be its excuse for being. In my travels in this country, ever since I left New York City, in the winter of 1893, and during the years of my ministry in the Middle West and in Boston, I was called upon on numerous occasions to tell the story of my life. I told this story, in brief, at many church and club meetings, before schools and at hospitable firesides, never thinking that it possessed any greater merits than to entertain an audience for the space of an hour, or give an interested group of friends the pleasure of a rather novel conversation.

In the summer of 1912, while on a visit to the famous summer resort, Manchester-By-the-Sea, Massachusetts, I was entertained at a beautiful and hospitable home where the gracious members of the family requested me to

tell them my "interesting story." Deeming the
narrative worthy to be published, they brought
it to the attention of the editor of the *Atlantic
Monthly*. In that highly esteemed magazine,
under the general title, "A Far Journey,"
several chapters of this autobiography appeared, and are here reprinted (with much new
material added) by courtesy of the editor.

This narrative's excuse for being is, I believe,
to be found, first, in the fact that it is the story,
not of an individual, but of a type. There are
many others of the children of other lands who
have come to the New World as learners of the
modes of life and thought of a superior people;
who have succeeded in discovering America on
its ideal side, and who know and love this
country as that Commonwealth of free, enlightened, and beneficent citizens. Second, this
story justifies its existence by being a testi-
mony to the unparalleled opportunities of
America. Here, as nowhere else on this planet,
the "talented foreigner" finds the ample room
and noble incentives necessary to reveal his

PREFACE

talents and to enable him to attain the more abundant intellectual, political, social, and moral life.

While writing the earlier chapters of this story I often seemed to myself to be portraying another life than my own; the periods of childhood and youth appeared to belong to a remote order of things definitely detached from the one in which I now find myself. Yet, in a large sense, the impassable gulf between my Syrian life and my American life is only seeming, and not real. I am conscious of no loss of continuity. Just as manhood *fulfills* rather than *destroys* childhood, so does America's large, tumultuous life tend to realize the possibilities with which the ancient, mystic, dreamy Orient endowed me. So to Syria, my loving, untutored mother, as to America, my virile, resourceful teacher, I offer my profound and lasting gratitude.

A. M. R.

Boston, Massachusetts.

CONTENTS

ILLUSTRATIONS

[xiii]

ILLUSTRATIONS

A FAR JOURNEY

A FAR JOURNEY

CHAPTER I

MY FATHER'S HOUSE

WHEN I first came into this world the Rihbany clan experienced the usual rejoicing which comes to a Syrian clan when a man-child is born to one of its families. My kindred rejoiced at my advent, not merely because I was a son instead of a daughter, important as that was, but because I was an asset of the clan, a possible reinforcement to their fighting strength, which they had to use often against another powerful clan in the town, called Jirdak. In the Jirdak camp, however, a correspondingly great sorrow was felt. On the same night on which I was born they lost by death one of their most valiant fighters. To be so reduced in power at the same time that the enemy was reinforced with a possible fighter, seemed to the Jirdaks to be a stern heavenly visitation which it was beyond their ability to bear. But so far as I was concerned, the enemies of my people sorrowed in vain. I never lifted a finger against them, never had the chance. My years of strength find me fighting greater battles far, far away from them, but not with carnal weapons.

The usual formalities were observed on the occasion of my birth. Friends, both men and women, came to our house in large numbers, into the very room where the day-old babe and its mother lay, to extend their congratulations. They brought their presents with them as did the "Wise Men" of old on their historic visit to Bethlehem. They sang and were exceeding glad, because unto them a child was born, a son was given. They were served with wine, coffee, and confections. I was baptized by triple immersion, in the name of the Father, Son, and Holy Ghost, and thus adopted by the holy and ancient Greek Orthodox Church as one of her children. When I was forty days old, my mother, being permitted again to come into the sanctuary, carried me to the door of the church, as is the custom, where the robed priest met her, took me in his arms, as the aged Simeon took the infant Jesus, and presented me at the altar before the God of my fathers. In our family history I took rank as the fourth of a family of twelve children, five sons and seven daughters.

My parents were illiterate, as were their parents before them, and the parents of their parents, for generations. My father was a stone-mason, a contractor and builder. He was a man of simple, unaffected dignity, kind-hearted, remarkably industrious, and devoted to his family. He was highly respected by his kindred and business associates throughout his life. He always seemed to me to be the type of man who would never willfully and designedly "walk in the counsel of the ungodly, nor stand in the way of sinners, nor sit in the seat of the scornful." In a business way, however, he was not of the truly sagacious type. Through a wily and decidedly unscrupulous uncle of his, he became involved in certain financial transactions which kept him in debt and perpetual anxiety from early manhood until near his death at the age of eighty. And, oh, that "debt," and the ever-recurring dread "interest" at twelve per cent, and the thousand things which my father might have done to escape the evil designs of his uncle! How they haunted my soul from infancy to manhood, and how I shiver and shrink even now when I recall them to mind! Every bit of our property was taken away from us by the "Frenchman" who held the mortgage and the hated "note," after my father had struggled for years, at least to reduce the debt, but was prevented from doing so by the exorbitant rate of interest he was forced to pay.

My mother was in some respects more richly endowed by nature than my father. I grew up to consider her the intellectual leader of the family. She possessed an alert and resourceful mind, was swift both to hear and to speak, humorous, and generous to a fault. In our family troubles we generally looked to mother for the wisest counsel. Along with her intellectual endowment, she possessed beauty of face and form, and absolute fearlessness. I never knew my mother to fear any situation, or anybody. Only the "debt" oppressed her, because it was foisted upon my father by others. Those who knew her father always testified that she inherited his fearless spirit.

From description, I should judge that that grandfather of mine was such a man as Gideon, or Othniel, or Samson of the ancient leaders of Israel. His mighty voice was so heartening to his own clan in battle, and so terrifying to the enemy, that he was known to his generation as "Ibrahim the Tiger." My mother never forgot to remind me, with "great expectations," of the fact that I bore her father's name. She said that his sister picked me up when I was but an hour old, kissed my doughy, wrinkly, primitive face, and named me Ibrahim (Abraham), but, rather fortunately, left out "the tiger." Her action was confirmed at my baptism.

My mother's strength of mind and great courage did not, as is sometimes the case with such women, militate against her feminine qualities. She was always a woman from the tip of her finger to the center of her heart, and according to the fashion of her time and country an excellent housekeeper.

My father's house was a typical, common, Syrian house. It was one story high, and consisted of two rooms, a living-room and a store-room. It was built of roughly hewn stone,[1] and had one door and two windows, which had wooden shutters, without glass. The roof was the Biblical earth-covered flat roof, such as the one on which Peter went up to pray in ancient Joppa. On every Syrian roof there is a stone roller, with which the dirt is rolled down and made hard enough to "shed water." "Rolling the roof" is a daily task for the man of the house in the winter season. Failure to do this causes the roof to soften and the rain to soak through and "drop" into the house. The "dropping" is one of the most hateful things to

[1] In the western part of Syria all the houses are built of stone; in the eastern part, generally of sun-dried brick.

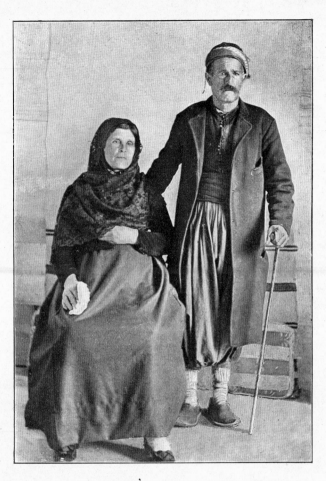

A. M. RIHBANY'S FATHER AND MOTHER

a Syrian household. The writer of the book of Proverbs did not at all exaggerate the ugliness of the situation when he said, "Continual dropping in a very rainy day and a contentious woman are alike."

The interior of that house of my early childhood appears on the negative of my memory in this shape: On the right as you enter stands a small structure of sun-dried brick, called *mekhdaah*. It is about five feet high, six feet long, and a foot deep. On the inner side it is divided into openings of different sizes, and serves the cosmopolitan purpose of a china closet, kettle cupboard, a place for father's Turkish pipe (*narghile*) and tobacco, and whatever other little articles it may be convenient for the moment to thrust into it. The *maukedah* (fireplace) is at the forward end of this structure. It is such a fireplace as you would build at a picnic: square, open at the top for the kettle to set in, and at one side to admit the fuel. It is built of clay mixed with straw and fine quartz. There is no chimney. The smoke floats in the house

[9]

with the sufferance of public opinion. The ceiling is black and shining as if it had been varnished. The earthen floor is painted frequently with red mud, and rubbed with a smooth stone until it shines. It is furnished with straw mats, cushions, and, in the winter season, soft and fluffy sheepskins. There are no chairs, no bedsteads. The family sit and sleep on the floor. The bed consists of a thick cushion for a mattress, stuffed with wool or cotton, a pillow of the same material, and a quilt for a cover. So when Jesus said to the man he had healed, "Arise, take up thy bed and walk," the man did not have very much to carry. In the daytime the beds are either rolled up, each one in a heap, and left on the floor, next to the wall, or put into a recess in the wall, constructed for the purpose.

By the stone pillar stands the large earthen barrel of flour, on top of which is the large basin in which the bread is kept. Back, by the partition which stands between the two rooms, are two or three large, plain wooden chests which form the wardrobe for the whole family. The opposite wall contains many openings in which earthen jars, containing the family winter supply of dried fruits, cereals, butter, lentils, beans, crushed wheat, olives, olive oil, molasses, rice, and other earthly comforts, are placed. By the door, on the left, there is a low wooden bench which holds the fresh-water jars, in which the women of the house carry the water from the fountain, as did the woman of Samaria whom Jesus met at Jacob's well. There are no pictures on the whitewashed walls. The only ornaments are a shotgun, an ammunition belt, a short sword, and a few articles of wearing apparel, which hang from wooden nails. There are no books of any kind, no musical instruments. The other room contains the wood and charcoal, tools, and so forth.

My father's house did not stand on a street, because streets are unknown to Syrian towns. There was no lawn around the house, no fence, no garden of any kind, no flower-beds. The immediate surroundings were our grove of mulberry trees, consisting of four large terraces, a terrace of grapevines, a large fig tree which bore black figs, a pomegranate tree, and an apple tree. On the west side of the house we had a large climbing rosebush, which lifted its flaming top above the roof, and an alder bush, which bore blossoms of delicate texture and sweet fragrance. These bushes were permitted to share the soil with the more useful trees, not simply for æsthetic delight, but because their blossoms possessed medicinal properties. At least we thought so, and thoughts are things. The houses of my two uncles, father's brothers, stood very near our house, and had similar surroundings.

Back of our house, and extending some three hundred feet eastward, stood a row of majestic oak trees, which did not belong to us. They were perfect specimens of strength and beauty, and a real delight to the senses and the soul. But, strange as this may seem, the proximity of those trees to our house and my uncles' houses was very displeasing to our families. In so poor a country as Syria has been for ages, objects of mere intellectual and æsthetic delight savor of vain and vexatious things. The mode of life is severely utilitarian. Only the rich and the Europeans revel in the pleasures of gardens and other great luxuries. To the masses, the only desirable possessions are those things which can be converted into bread and raiment. The owners of those oak trees were of the families more highly favored with the things of this world; therefore they did not need the revenue which the strip of land occupied by the oak trees might yield, if put to better use.

But our family felt differently about this matter. The oaks shaded a whole terrace of our precious, silk-yielding mulberry trees, and some grapevines, while their mighty roots drained the soil of its substance. That was a grave situation. It meant for us loss of revenue. The mighty oaks assumed in the eyes of my people the functions of highway robbers, of enemies which never slumbered nor slept and which stood at our very door. How to get rid of them was one of those family perplexities which filled my childish mind with disquieting curiosity. My father was offered much advice, gratis, as to how to kill those pernicious oaks. Not being ours, they had, of course, to be killed in some mysterious way. One of my uncles, who was of a rather grasping disposition, felt a decidedly keener antagonism toward the oaks than did my father. At times he looked and swore at them with great avidity.

So far as I can remember, the first means which was employed to wither those giants of the forest was prayer, the Oriental's most natural speech. But, for some reason or other, prayer failed to accomplish the desired results. Then an appeal was addressed to St. John (I do not recall whether it was the Baptist or the Evangelist), whose convent was in full view from our house, farther down on the slope of the hill. He was promised three piasters (twelve cents) and a cruse of pure olive oil to be burned in the lamp which hung in front of his very picture. The understanding was that the saint was to show signs of death in the oaks before any payment was made; but St. John, for reasons known only to himself, failed to rise to the occasion and do what was expected. That was a severe disappointment.

However, there were other means of relief yet to be tried. My father was advised to seek a magician and have him "blast" the oaks by his diabolical art. The formula as I heard it stated was this: The magician would enchant a pailful of water; breathe into it the very essence of Satan himself. Then all my father had to do was to step out in the night and sprinkle the enchanted water at the trunks of the oak trees, close to the ground, and they would wither in an incredibly short time. Fortunately for the trees, however, such magicians passed through our town only at long and uncertain intervals, and when one of them happened to be at hand, father was either absent from home, or something else happened to make the moment altogether inopportune for such dangerous operations.

One of our cousins urged that an appeal be

made to a person having the "evil eye." One
having the evil eye was supposed to do great
damage by just admiring an object. A fat and
sweet baby, a handsome and strong man, a
beautiful woman, a very fruitful tree, an abundant crop of silk cocoons, or any other good and
beautiful person or thing, stood in constant
danger of being injured or even killed by an
admiring evil eye. Often did my mother grab
and run away with me — her beautiful baby —
to the nearest hiding-place, when one who was
supposed to "strike with the eye " happened
to be passing anywhere near our house. Certainly those oak trees were things to be ad-
mired. Then why not secure an evil-eyed person, and bribe him or her to cast upon those
trees a blasting look? However, those persons
who were suspected of having the evil eye, for
obvious reasons never would admit the fact,
and certainly they were not in the market for
hire.

The last prescription to be considered, so far
as I remember, for doing away with the beauti-

ful oaks, was the use of mercury. Father was
told by those who "knew," that if he would
take an auger and bore a hole in any tree and
then pour in the hole a small quantity of mercury — "live mercury" — the tree would die.
Mercury, being very heavy in weight and of
such awful, mysterious potency, would pene-
trate the fibers of the tree in seeking to return
to the ground, course through the roots, and
thus destroy all their fibers. That was a simple
operation. But father was not the kind of a
man to undertake it. He might resort to some
impersonal agency of destruction, like prayer
or magic, but to do evil himself, to destroy with
his own hands, that he would not. He would
not assassinate a tree any more than he would
a person. So far as I know, the oak trees still
stand, and wave their lofty tops over the mulberry trees and the grapevines which were
forced away from us by my father's creditors.

It must be that the nights I was first aware
of in my father's house made deeper impres-

sions upon my mind than the days, because
they offer themselves now to my pen as the
earliest bits of my conscious existence, — this,
I suppose, because of the fear with which they
inspired me. I do not recall the time when, as a
little child, those deep shadows which the dim
lamplight emphasized behind the pillar in the
middle of the house, and other objects, did not
frighten me whenever I looked at them. Our
only source of light was a small kerosene lamp,
one of the very first to come to our town after
the subtle fluid of the Standard Oil Company
reached Syria, shortly before my conscious life
began. It was, however, a great improvement
on the little olive-oil lamp, the "candle" of the
Sermon on the Mount and the Ten Virgins —
an earthen saucer, with a protruding little lip
curled up at one point in the rim for the wick.
The lamp was placed on the edge of the *mekhdaah*, just above the fireplace. The corner in its
immediate vicinity was reasonably well lighted,
but the remoter parts of the living-room were
veiled with ghastly yellowish darkness.

But the most vivid of my early memories of kerosene is very grim. In filling the lamp one night my sister spilled some oil on the earthen floor. In order to amuse me she told me to soak little bits of cloth in the oil and touch a match to them and they would burn quickly. As I was doing so one of the little rags fell from my hand on the floor. I thought I saw where it fell and reached down and grabbed something that looked like it. It was a scorpion! The fiery sting pierced my flesh under the thumb nail. I rolled on the floor, a ball of quivering flesh, with a dart of the bitterest, fiery pain, which never abated the whole night, reaching from my thumb to my heart.

I feel no hesitancy in saying that when Rehoboam said to the people of Israel, "My father chastised you with whips but I will chastise you with scorpions," he made a telling figure, and the people of that country, which is full of all manner of "creeping things," must have understood him very clearly.

Our nights were not tricked into cheerfulness

by any of the multitude of means which delight
child-life in this age and country. As a child I
enjoyed the love and care of devoted parents,
the deep, instinctive, but untutored affections
and protection of a richly endowed mother.
But notwithstanding all that, and except on
festive occasions, the evenings were very dreary
for the little ones. There were no children's
story-books to read, and there was no one who
could have read them, if any of them had fallen
into our hands: no pictures for the children,
and none to cheer the blankness of those whitewashed walls, which the smoke tinged with a
murky hue: no toys of any kind. Now and then
we fell spontaneously into a fit of laughter, or
played a game of hide-and-seek in the dark
corners of the room. Now and then we were
favored with a tale about a miracle happening
in the graveyard, or about ghosts, or wild
beasts, which made the very hairs of our heads
hiss with fear. Our peevishness and naughtiness
had no "psychological guidance." When
bribes, which were by no means of the most

persuasive kind, failed, the chief remedy was,
"Be good or the camel will get you!" "Listen!
the hyena is coming!—*Coming! right at the
door!!*" From the fact that men could ride on
his back, we always concluded that the camel
must possess at least the imitation of a human
spirit. But the hyena, so terrible and so abundant in the surrounding woods and rocky hills,
never failed to bring us to terms. This is why,
I believe, my earliest memories of the nights
in my father's house claim precedence as I
write.

And as I reflect on those days now, I realize
most clearly how limited, how meagerly inventive, is love without culture. How almost helpless is sympathy without knowledge. Love is,
indeed, "the greatest thing in the world," but
without knowledge, acquired knowledge, —
real culture, — love is like a skilled workman
without his tools, a mariner without his chart
and compass.

But the more joyful memories of those plastic
years were stored in my mind in the spring and

the summer seasons, when the trees poured out
their riches in tender leaves and blossoms.
In Syria the seasons do not forget to come on
time; the calendar and nature are in perfect
harmony. There are no "raw winds" and no
"cold showers" in April and May. Rain very
rarely falls between April and September. The
myriads of white and yellow daisies are already
out in full force in the latter part of April, and
we children rolled on the fragrant blossoms as
on a thick carpet. We plucked the daisies and
strung them by the yard for necklaces and belts.
When the ploughman came to plough the mulberry terraces for us, I experienced a delicious
sensation. When that rough peasant arrived
with his primitive plough on his right shoulder,
the yoke hanging from the left shoulder, his
long, hard, strong goad — the same as the one
with which "Shamgar, son of Anath, slew of
the Philistines six hundred men" — in his left
hand, and his two cows, or oxen, or cow and ox,
walking before him, my childish eyes beheld
a most enchanting picture. His "laborer" also

THE PLOUGHMAN

came with the ploughman to break the clods
behind the plough. "Judah shall plough, and
Jacob shall break the clods." I would stand at
a respectful distance, because of their menacing
horns, and, with joyous bewilderment, watch
those cows, with their eyes enlarged and their
backs kinked, pull at the urging and goading
of their master, turn the soil and cause the
small stones and clods to roll musically over
the terrace walls.

In the latter part of April also the eggs or
"seeds" of the silkworm [1] begin to stir with life
in the muslin sack (their winter quarters) hanging from the ceiling. A scaffolding of poles and
long, strong reeds is built along the entire wall-
space in the house, and clear up to the ceiling.
The trays which should hold the silkworms
are placed on the scaffolding in rows and tiers,
and the *mousam* — silkworm season — begins.
Mother takes the sack of eggs down, as she
makes the sign of the cross and implores the

[1] In the western part of Syria the silk crop is the
people's chief source of livelihood.

divine blessing on the silk crop that is to be. The sack is opened, and a few tiny, almost microscopic worms are seen to quiver among the dull gray eggs. A tender mulberry leaf is placed in the sack, on which the little worms soon gather. The leaf is lifted out with its precious freight and placed on a tray, where the worms proceed to receive regular rations. Leaf after leaf thus proceeds into and out of the sack, until all the "blessed ones" are transferred to the trays. As they grow larger the lots on the trays are divided and subdivided until the whole house is filled with bright, greedy, unspeakably interesting silkworms. Holy water is secured from the priest, consecrated especially to protect the crop from ants and mice, and sprinkled on the lower terminus of every pole in the scaffolding. With such a sense of security we proceed to bestow tender and incessant care on the silkworms, for forty days, at which time they cease to eat and begin to spin their cocoons in the bundles of brush especially prepared for them.

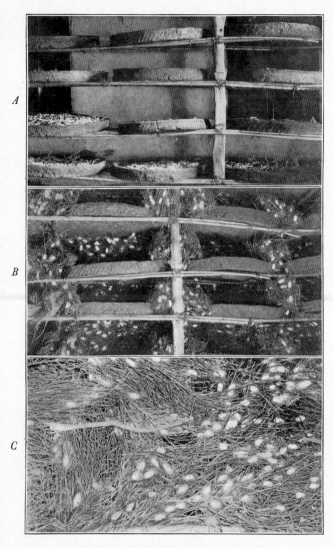

A. Ready to spin; B. Ready for Harvest; C. A Luxuriant Yield

SILK WORMS AND COCOONS

MY FATHER'S HOUSE

Oh, how delightful it is to watch those precious worms weave their silken envelopes. Thousands of them are at work. The web is fastened to a suitable nook in the brush; the upper half of the worm's body sways rhythmically and, seemingly, understandingly; the thread, proceeding from the little black mouth, is thrown round and round as far as the little body can reach. A haze of a web is formed. It is white, yellow, or yellowish brown. My eyes feast on the scene for hours. The web grows heavier; the weaver is barely visible, — it is all hid! In a week's time the bundles of brush are converted into a solid mass of cocoons. One of the most luxurious of the bundles is given to the patron saint of the family for his gracious protection of the crop. Some choice cocoons are saved for seed, and the rest of the crop is sold to the spinners.

The *mousam* over, the housewife proceeds to the annual whitewashing of the walls of the house and the mending and repolishing of the earthen floor. If she is not obliged to seek

the hills herself and secure the needed *tarsh* —
chalky white earth — she buys a penny's worth
of the stuff from one of the men who peddle it
early in the season. The enterprising woman
dissolves the *tarsh* in a large basinful of water,
and very dexterously slaps the liquid on the
walls of the house with a piece of sheepskin.
As much of the substance in proportion as
adheres to the wall rebounds on the woman,
who, after a few hours of "slapping," assumes
the appearance of a veritable "pillar of salt."

I always looked forward to this performance
as to a holiday. In the absence of the motion-
picture show, the merry-go-round, and any
other juvenile entertainment, whitewashing
the house afforded the youngsters the stimulus
of a significant change in the routine of life,
which for the time being enhanced the circulation of the nervous energy. It was real
"fun" to haul out all the furniture from the
house to the terrace, dispose the earthen barrels, huge jars and clothes-chests in the shape
of temporary defenses around the spot where

the beds were spread, and sleep for a night or two out under the winking stars. My parental grandmother had the faculty of reserving most of her harrowing stories for such nights, when she told them with the ease of an expert, "just to entertain me." But as the common people of Syria believe that each person has a star in heaven which holds the mysteries of his destiny, I often strayed from my grandmother's stories by gazing at the luminous dome above, curious to know which of the countless trembling stars was mine. My choice often fell upon a real bright orb.

The summer, always known to us as "the time of grapes and figs," follows and I dance for joy. Our own vines and fig trees — the desire of a peaceful Israel — are laden with fruit. We have red, white, and black grapes. Our fig trees bear white, black, yellow, green, and purple figs. The black fig tree is nearest to the house, and I practically nest in it during the fig season. I love to see the delicious ripe figs show their African faces among the large, rough, green leaves. I rise in the cool of the morning, before the sun has lifted the dew on high, and proceed to the beneficent fig tree. A "shred" of bread[1] and all the fresh figs I can eat besides make up my breakfast. I never knew in those days what indigestion was. The grapes and pomegranates afford delightful varieties. My uncle has an apricot tree near the house. He instructs me "not to touch it," but I do, both for the sake of eating apricots, and to spite him. Early in the autumn we store the dried fruits, vegetables, and cereals in jars and earthen barrels and make ready for the winter.

That was my father's house in its natural setting and human atmosphere. That was the feeding-place and shrine of my early childhood, and these are my memories of it.

[1] Syrian loaves are generally made round and as thin as thick wrapping-paper. In weight a loaf equals a large-sized roll.

CHAPTER II

EL-SHWEIR

The larger environment of my early years was the town of El-Shweir in which my father's house stood. El-Shweir falls, geographically, in the province of Mount Lebanon, Syria, in Asiatic Turkey. It is situated about midway between Jerusalem on the south, and Antioch on the north, about sixty miles to the northwest of Damascus, and fifteen miles east of Beyrout and the Mediterranean Sea. Ecclesiastically, El-Shweir falls within the ancient See of Antioch, in the chief city of which the followers of Christ were first called "Christians."

From the time when I first became able to understand an ordinary conversation, until I emigrated to America at the age of twenty-two, I was always told, and therefore learned to assert myself, that the town of my birth was an impregnable stronghold. El-Shweir never was walled or fortified. The confidence of the inhabitants in its impregnability springs from the fact that the town is built on the lower slopes of high, rocky hills which inclose a deep, horse-shoe-shaped gorge. The "military" strategists of El-Shweir have always asserted, with the authority of the men of their class, that musketeers could shoot much more effectively when aiming upward than when aiming downward. Therefore an enemy approaching the town from the commanding heights was by necessity of his position at a decided disadvantage. The much more steady upward firing of the defenders was sure to scatter his forces and put him to flight. The reassuring tradition still survives in that community that even Ibrahim Pasha, the famous Egyptian conqueror, remarked more than once, during his Syrian campaign in his war against Turkey, that El-Shweir could not be taken by an invading enemy, however strong. Whatever military value this opinion may or may not have, pragmatically speaking, it "worked" mightily by lending the inhabitants of our town a strong sense of security. And, furthermore, the fact stands sublimely convincing that (I suppose because no enemy has ever tried to take it) El-Shweir has never been taken by an enemy.

The rocky hills which surround El-Shweir are crowned with lofty pine trees, the lower slopes are covered with grapevines and fig trees, while groves of mulberry trees form the immediate environs of the town. In its depressed location the only view El-Shweir enjoys of the outside world is the majestic elevation of one of the two highest peaks of Western Lebanon, called Sunnin, which rises about nine thousand feet above sea-level. Ascending to the summits of the surrounding hills, however, one beholds some of the most beautiful and sublime natural scenery in the world: the rugged and picturesque slopes of Western Lebanon, terminating in luxurious gardens at the sandy shores of the blue and dreamy Mediterranean; the city of Beyrout, with its white buildings standing on the glittering shore like blocks of silver on a cloth of gold; a countless number of hills and mountains, groves of pine and olive trees, winding streams, vineyards, and a multitude of towns and hamlets, nestling in the bosom of the hills in all directions as far as the eye can see.

The inhabitants of El-Shweir, who are supposed to count ten thousand, — and to the poetic Oriental mind a supposition is always more agreeable than an actual count, — are all of the Christian faith, and overwhelmingly Greek Orthodox. The minority consists of Maronites and Greek Catholics.[1] The inhab-

---

[1] The Greek Orthodox Church, known also as the Eastern Church, includes a great portion of Christendom, and with the exception of the Russian dominions is governed by the four independent patriarchs of Constantinople, Alexandria, Antioch, and Jerusalem.

The Maronite Church is an ancient national communion of Mount Lebanon, which in the twelfth century came voluntarily under the sway of the Pope of Rome. It is governed by a local patriarch and a hierarchy, and retains many of its ancient characteristics, such as the marriage of the inferior clergy and the use of the Syriac service.

The Greek Catholic Church is a branch of the Greek Orthodox Church, which, as the result of a schism,

itants' chief source of livelihood is the stone-mason trade, which is handed down from father to son, not, however, according to status, but from choice. The majority of the men follow this trade, and the minority provide the town with its storekeepers, blacksmiths, carpenters, butchers, muleteers and loafers — the leisure class.

The large majority of the houses of El-Shweir were similar to our house. A few houses were two stories, and one or two three stories high. There were no streets. Syrian towns never were built according to preconceived plans. Each man built on his own piece of land, regardless of general convenience and symmetry. One or two main roads ran winding through the town, and crooked stony footpaths, running from all directions, connected with those roads. In the rainy season the roads became streams

joined the Church of Rome in the eighteenth century. The chief "Western" characteristics of this church are its submission to the Pope and its adoption of the Gregorian Calendar. In other respects it is practically the same as the Greek Orthodox Church.

of water, mud and slush, and pedestrians picked their way as best they could.

The Orient in general has never troubled itself about sanitation, not even in the large cities. At the present time some changes for the better are gradually being introduced, but in my early years the country was just as Isaiah and Paul left it. Filth and refuse were thrown everywhere in the roads and around the houses. The "dung-hill" existed by every house. The people knew nothing about germs, and the germs apparently knew nothing about the people. Or rather, the germs did their utmost with the people generations ago, leaving only those who proved germ-proof.

In recent years El-Shweir has made some progress in certain directions, but when I was a child it was decidedly primitive. When I think of that portion of my life in comparison with my present state, I seem to myself to have traveled through the lights and shadows of two thousand years. I never knew in those days what a library was; never saw street lights, glass windows, iron stoves, public halls, newspapers, structural iron of any kind, or anything that rolled on wheels. I had never heard the piano but once (in the home of an American missionary) before I came to America. Public education, citizenship, a national flag, political institutions of any description, were as unknown to me as the postulated inhabitants of Mars.

The social life of the El-Shweir of my childhood was no less strangely interesting. As in other parts of Syria, and as in the days of Israel and Canaan, and the Jews and the Samaritans, the various clans of the town lived on terms of mutual enmity. Seldom did a year pass without a serious fight occurring between the clan of Rihbany and the clan of Jirdak. To down the other clans seemed to be every clan's ideal. This I was taught by example and precept from my infancy. Often did I hear a cousin of mine say that he would pay the toll-tax for every man who died in the clan of Jirdak. As clans, we lived in accordance with the precept, "Eye for eye, tooth for tooth, burning for burning, wound for wound," and no favor. There was indeed social intercourse between the various clans; there were common feasts and festivals. But all these were temporary concessions which our contiguous existence and the oneness of our religious faith required. It is not difficult to see, therefore, that under such conditions the ideal man for us was the fighter. The good man, the man wise in counsel, was indeed greatly revered, but he needed the fighter to maintain his supremacy.

Of these thoughts my young soul drank its fill. Those men of strong limbs, heavy voices, and fiery eyes stood for me as the heights of my climbing ambition. To be like one of them was a dream which seemed to me too good to be realized. And those interclannish fights, which I witnessed in my innocent, plastic days, thrill my soul to its center, even now, when I think of them. The sight of a few hundred men engaged in a hand-to-hand fight, shouting, cursing, swearing, and inflamed with wrath; hundreds of women shrieking, children howling in terror; stones, clubs, and clods flying in all directions, blood dripping from heads and faces, was indeed bewildering, overwhelming for a little soul to witness.

But what must seem strange to an American is the fact that, considering the large number of men engaged and the duration of the fight, the injuries caused by those interclannish combats were rather slight. Very few men ever were seriously injured, and rarely, if ever, any one killed. The reason of this was that those men, as a rule, fought like big boys, seeking simply to "humble" one another. They had no great issues at stake. The causes of such quarrels were most often very trivial. Two women of different clans might quarrel at the public fountain over the question as to whose turn it was to fill her jar first, and thus precipitate a fight. Two men, each championing the cause of a mythical hero, fall into serious disputing. "Your 'hero' was a coward," says the one. "You, your hero, and all your clan are cowards," says the other. "Say no such words against my clan," retorts the angry opponent; "did we not tread on your necks at the last fight? Just remember that day and plaster your mouth shut." Of course nothing more is needed to plunge two clans into a fight. Again a similar situation might be created by two boys fighting in like fashion; or at a funeral when a dispute arises as to what clan has the right to lift the bier first and start it on its way to the sepulcher; or at the game of "tossing the ball," or "lifting the mortar" (see below), or any other trivial occurrence, coming just at the "right time."

Such being very often the causes of those fights, the men, as a rule, sought merely to "down the foe" and humiliate him by "treading on the necks"[1] of their antagonists. Thus we read in the Book of Joshua, when the "five kings," of Jerusalem, Hebron, Jarmuth,

[1] This expression is meant often to signify victory, even if the "treading on the neck" does not actually take place.

Lachish, and Eglon, were brought out of the cave, "that Joshua called for all the men of Israel, and said unto the captains of the men of war which went with him, Come near, put your feet on the necks of these kings. And they came near, and put their feet on the necks of them." That was the most exalted symbol of victory for Israel.

But clannish life has its decidedly romantic side. Provided one is able and willing to forget the larger interests of civilization and the nobler visions of nationalism and human brotherhood, and make the rule of his social life the faulty maxim, "My clan, right or wrong," I know of no more delightful social state than that which clannish life affords. As I write, the past rises before me like a bewitching dream. I am carried back to the time when the hearts of all my kinsmen throbbed, beat for beat, with my heart; when every one of their homes was as much mine as my own fireside, when we lived in life's shifting lights and shadows, "all for each and each for all." The fact that we dwelt among antagonistic clans served only to heighten our heroism, strengthen our clannish cohesion, and intensify the delightfulness of our kinship.

A clan gathering is itself a feast. When the "men of counsel and the men of war" meet together, not in a public hall, but at the home of an "*aam*" (uncle or kinsman) for the purpose of "reconciling" a family feud, or negotiating a marriage, or planning how to meet an impending danger, each man feels that his strength is that of a hundred. The small cups of Turkish coffee are passed, first to the oldest and most honored man present, and then to the others according to age, married men taking precedence over the unmarried. They all drink, and, as each one places back on the tray his empty cup and its beaten-brass holder, with the right hand lifted toward the forehead, he says to the host, "May we always drink coffee in your hospitable home [meaning, "May you always be able thus to entertain"] in times of joy and gladness"; and to the youth who passes the coffee, "May we drink it again at your wedding." So far as its large interests are concerned the clan is a unit. It may "withdraw" from him who refuses to abide by its decisions, and thus render him a social outcast. "That soul shall be cut off from his people."

The large majority of the men of El-Shweir were absent from their homes from spring until late autumn. As a rule they left their home town right after the Easter festival, and scattered all over Syria in pursuit of their trade as stone-masons. In their travels "in the land of the stranger" they forgot their clannish animosities and worked and lived together as friends. They stored their summer wages in their Damascus-made girdles, until their return home. Their families in the mean time lived on credit.

Late in the autumn the men returned to town to spend the winter at home in complete idleness. Upon their arrival clannish animosities reasserted themselves in their hearts. Their wives, who stayed at home the year round and kept up their own feminine clannish fights, hardly allowed their returning husbands time enough to put their shoes from off their feet at the door, and their traveling-bags from off their backs, before they told them of the many indignities which had been heaped upon their families in their absence, not only by the women and children of the other clan, but also by the old men who remained in the town during the summer. Thus a grave situation was immediately created, and the men made ready to "clear for action" on short notice.

When my father came home the occasion was deliciously interesting to me. Life took on greater vigor and exhilaration. He brought with him many goodies which were "pleasant to the sight and good for food." The sound of the bubbling water in his long-idle *narghile*, the smell of the Persian tobacco smoked in it, his manly voice, and the sense of added security which his presence gave, were choice pleasures. It was a supreme moment for me when he took down the gun from the wall to clean and oil it. I was always taught that the gun was made by

SYRIAN BEAUTIES

Satan, and I should not touch it, but I never knew the time when I did not take awe-inspiring delight in looking at this product of Satan's genius.

The social pleasures of the people of our town were very simple and unlearned. No literary circles, no lectures, theaters, or receptions; no dried-beef-and-creamed-potato church suppers, or ice-cream socials to pay the minister's salary. The social routine was very simple and most favorable to the perpetuation of the juvenile temper. Life did not radiate in broad, intellectual, æsthetic, ethical, and political highways. It had only a few hungers to feed and small ambitions to satisfy. The inhabitants of the town gathered in homogeneous groups and feasted themselves on gossip and tales of adventure. Eating and drinking in parties was frequent. "Tossing the ball" was a favorite game with the men, which, however, frequently ended in a serious fight. "Lifting the mortar" was another heroic feat. A wooden handle was fastened in the hollow of a large stone mortar, and the strong men vied with one another in lifting it with the right arm to the shoulder, or the full height of the arm. Rivalry in this game, also, often precipitated a fight.

The game called "Two-steps-and-a-jump" was an exciting one. A "mark" was placed at a certain point. The player made a short run — "to gather his strength" — until he reached the mark. Then he sprang forward with all his might, two steps and a jump. Another mark was placed where his feet last struck the ground. Thus the men strove to out-distance one another, and he whose agility placed the second mark beyond the reach of all others won the day.

The coming of "the bear and the monkey" greatly excited the populace. The owner of the animals beat upon his tambourine at a certain spot in the town, to which the multitude hastened. A small sum was granted him by the authorities, out of the tax-money. He made the bear "dance" and the monkey perform antics. He sang songs, the enchanting qualities of which made the animals do certain pleasing things. But the climax of the bear-and-monkey entertainment was reached when some strong man offered to wrestle with the bear.

The man comes forward. The bear, urged by his owner, stands up on his hind feet. The wild and the human beast come together. The man's arms encircle the bear just under the armpits. The owner must see to it that the bear does not bite his antagonist. The battle is joined. The bear snorts and grunts. The man does no less. The crowd sways with every movement of the combatants. The owner urges his bear to victory. The crowd, in a similar manner, stiffen the resolution of the man. Such a battle cannot last long. The bear grows weaker, because he has danced long before the fight. The crowd shouts. The man grips the ground with his feet and, with a last mighty push, lands upon the roaring animal! Men rush forward, extricate the victor from the claws of the angry beast, and proclaim him hero. The owner soothes the misfortune of his vanquished pet.

One of the most exciting masculine dances of Syria is the *debkah*. It is an ancient Arab dance which goes back to the early days of Israel. At this dance about a dozen men, nearly equal in stature, holding hands, stand in a curved line. One outside the line beats the tune on a timbrel. The bodies of the dancers sway rhythmically, now to right and left, now forward and backward, with the recurring short measures of the music. At brief, regular intervals the dancers stamp forcibly with the right foot extended forward, with a quick, vigorous "Yah-O-Yah!" Again the bodies sway, the song is repeated, the feet strike the ground, and again, until the men are fatigued. It was something after this fashion that the ancient clans of Israel danced around their rough altars, with shouts of "Hallelujah!— Praise ye Jah."

Playing cards was a prevalent pastime. Propounding riddles, like that which Samson propounded to the Philistines, was very popular. Ghost stories abounded. The miraculous workings of saints were often and reverently rehearsed; the relative strength of the various kings of Europe considered, mythical heroes extolled, etc., etc.

But the chief social event of the town, the summit of social joy to both old and young, was the marriage feast. I always looked forward to a marriage feast as do those who watch for the morning. Its tumultuous joys rolled within my soul like ocean waves. It was then that as a child I could do absolutely as I pleased. It was then that my pockets burst with plenty. Sugarplums, nuts, raisins, cakes, and other delicacies fell into my hands in great profusion. The singing, dancing, and sword-playing thrilled every nerve in me. Both in childhood and youth, *El-Airis* (marriage feast) was to me an expression comprehensive of multitudinous joy.

According to the ancient customs of Syria, which go back to that wedding of Cana of Galilee and ages beyond it, it is not a wedding day that is appointed, but a wedding festival, which extends over several days, during which time the whole town thinks of nothing else.

During the preceding week, a deputation on behalf of the bridegroom's family, and another on behalf of the bride's, visit all the chief homes of the various clans in the town and notify them of the coming event. This is the equivalent of an invitation to all the members of all the families. Whosoever will may come. Only unfriendly clans or families are omitted, and only such refuse to come, even if invited. The parable in the Gospel of St. Matthew of "a certain king, which made a marriage for his son, and sent forth his servants to call them that were bidden to the wedding, and they would not come," indicates this social peculiarity. The intention of the parable was to show the persistent antagonism of the Jews of the apostolic age to the Christian faith. Though they were "called" again and again, they would not come. To refuse an invitation to a marriage feast in Syria, excepting in case of a recent sorrow, is a sign of deep-seated enmity.

EL–SCHWEIR

His wedding day is the supremest day in a man's life. Marriage to the Syrian Christians is not only a holy sacrament, but an ideal to which all other ideals stand subordinate. The loveliest thing a guest can say to parents at the end of a meal is, "May we eat again within this house at the wedding of the dear grooms [i.e., sons]." Matrimonial expectations are affectionately expressed to boys from early childhood. Whatever service or courtesy a boy renders, he is repaid for it by saying to him, "May we serve at your wedding?"

The guests come to the wedding in large groups, of hundreds and of fifties, representing clans and houses. While yet a short distance from the bridegroom's house they begin singing in groups and in diverse tunes. A large company of the groom's clan rushes out to meet the approaching throng, with singing and shouts of joy. The two groups meet and merge together, making not only "a joyful noise," but a deafening roar. They march into the house and are met by those within, with similar manifestations of joy. Presently all singing ceases. The relatives of the bridegroom stand in a straight line, with him as its center and glory, facing their guests who have also fallen in line. The guests, speaking all together, say, "Blessed, O bridegroom, be your enterprise; May Allah bless you with many sons and a long life; Our joy this day is supreme." To which the relatives of the bridegroom respond in similar fashion: "May Allah bless your lives; May such events happen in your homes; May all your sons who are needy [of marriage] be so blessed and made happy. You have honored us by your coming!" The two parties thus give vent to their happy feelings, simultaneously causing a commotion resembling an artillery duel. Only an expert in the etiquette of the occasion is able to comprehend the meaning of the felicitations.

This part of the proceedings in the marriage festivities was always most thrilling to me. So many strong men, dressed in their best and many-colored garments, formed for me a rare picture of strength and beauty. My soul expanded and contracted with the rise and fall of their mighty voices. My heart beat tumultuously as the two crowds merged together in happy confusion. My supreme care was to be at a safe distance from the wild tread of those many strong limbs, and the fearful points of those swords flashing at the head of the procession.

Sunday is the last and greatest day of the wedding festivities. It is the day of the solemnizing of the marriage, and all the town is out. If the ceremony is to take place at the house, then the bride is brought to the house of the bridegroom as Rebekah was brought to Isaac's house, where the consecration takes place. But if at the church, as is most often the case, then both the bridegroom and the bride are escorted there by the multitude. "The bringing of the bride" from her father's house was a most interesting event to me as a child. Picked men are sent to "bring the bride," thus echoing the ancient custom of strong men forcing the bride away from her kindred. If the bridegroom is to be grave and reserved in his conversation, the bride is expected to be absolutely silent while the festivities last. She is not to open her eyes, either, excepting on rare occasions. Nor is she to close her eyes tightly. That would be humiliating crudeness. She has been instructed carefully to exercise her eyelids with lovely gentleness, until they just touch fringes, with no sign of effort, or stress. The "drooping eyelids" of the right kind of a bride are poetized by the Syrians as a superb example of bewitching loveliness.

What seemed like an inscrutable mystery to my little mind, on such an occasion, was the behavior of the bridegroom and the bride. Where did they get, all at once, such unapproachable dignity? Were they still such people as we are? Were they still my cousins? It did not seem possible. I could hardly believe my eyes when I saw them a few days after the wedding conducting themselves just like other people. The bridegroom's looks were no longer awe-inspiring. The bride's eyes were wide open, and the output of her organs of speech seemed unlimited.

Shortly after the arrival of the escorting party, who are immediately served with wine and confections, the bride is led from her bridal seat by women attendants and the closest male friends of the bridegroom. The etiquette of the country requires that she walk out of her father's house extremely slowly. On some occasions the walk of the bride from the innermost part of the room to the door consumes about half an hour. A decorated horse or mule is at the door, on whose back she is lifted by the strong men of the party. Another mule carries the bride's bed and clothes-chest, and the procession moves slowly toward the sanctuary, amidst great rejoicing. A large concourse of people escorts the bridegroom.

When the ceremony takes place in the night, the whole affair assumes a brilliant aspect. Sword-players, singers, "musicians," torch-bearers, and other merrymakers surround the bridegroom, and are distributed also along the procession. The housetops are filled with spectators, largely women and children. They shower on the procession rose-water, flowerwater, wheat (the symbol of fecundity), and confections. Waves of *zelagheet* (songs peculiar to women) float over the marching host. The procession moves with flashing swords, flaring lamps and torches, and an indescribable din of music and song. "Behold the bridegroom cometh! Go ye out to meet him," and woe to those "foolish virgins" who are not ready to join the joyous throng! The contracting parties meet at the altar, and are joined together in holy marriage by a most impressive ceremony. This done, the mighty host retraces its steps with the happy couple to the house of the bridegroom, where the chief feast of the occasion has been prepared. Food is provided for an unlimited number of guests. They come from all the walks of life, from "the highways and the hedges," and the house is literally filled. In the summer season the feast is spread on the housetop, but as most of the weddings occur

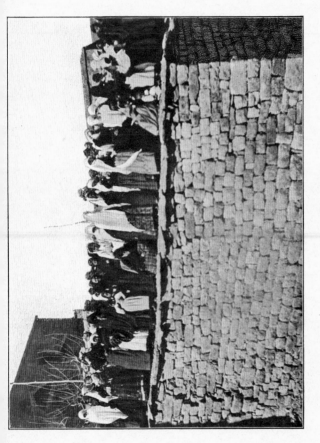

WATCHING FROM A HOUSETOP THE COMING OUT OF THE BRIDE

in the winter, the guests crowd into the house, and eat and drink from an apparently unlimited supply of Syrian generosity. With this feast end the wedding festivities.

Such were the simple pleasures and social activities amid which my earthly life began. So distressingly homogeneous, so unmixed with higher intellectual and ethical delights, was the life of my people.

But for justice' sake it should be stated here that the Syrians are as richly endowed with intellectual possibilities and social instincts as any people. Those of them who have had the privileges of a more highly organized social life and of higher education, especially in Europe and America, have amply shown their capacity to become highly educated and socially refined. But the history of Syria has been a series of misfortunes. As the battle-field of mighty empires from time immemorial, Syria has always been tossed from the hands of one tyrannical government to those of another, and deprived of all the agencies which make for enlightened nationalism. It has had no higher education to rid the mind of trivialities and superstitions, and lead to the higher unity of ideals; no industry to teach the value of time and create a longing for peace; no civic spirit to convert life's activities into ethical and social values, and lead to the love of law and order, and to cleanliness and beauty of material surroundings. There is at present a new spirit stirring in that country, and it is hoped that a new era may soon dawn upon that ancient mother of the greatest of religions in the possession of man, and give the nobler qualities of her children a fair chance to reveal and develop themselves.

Such was the home of my people when it was first introduced to my consciousness; out of it I have traveled by devious ways to the vastly various and complex present.

CHAPTER III

My intellectual history began in the school of my uncle, my mother's first and favorite cousin, Priest Michael, of the Holy and Apostolic Greek Orthodox Church. I could not have been much more than three years old when my mother led me to sit at the feet of the priest of my people and receive instruction. The "Child Mind," "School Age," "Adolescence," and the many other psychological zones were unknown to my people. I could say "papa" and "mamma," and many other words at the age of three, and according to my parents' ideas I might just as well be saying the letters of the alphabet.

At that time the men who could read and write in El-Shweir were extremely few. Certain parish priests established what might be called reading circles for the purpose of fitting some of the youth of the parish with sufficient knowledge of reading to assist the priest at the mass.

The course consisted of the alphabet, the Book of Psalms, writing, and a short exercise in mental arithmetic.

My recollections of my uncle's school are dim and meager. His house consisted of two rooms, one of which was the schoolroom. Besides the door this room had one window, which had wooden shutters and no glass. It was opened when the weather permitted.

The pupils, who numbered about twenty-five, sat on the straw mats on the floor with their legs crossed under them. In compliance with good manners, we took our shoes from off our feet upon entering the room, just outside the threshold in summer and just inside in winter. In the days of Moses that was done as a sign of reverence for holy places, as he did it before the "burning bush"; and, as in ancient Syria every family had a household god, the shoes had to be removed from the feet upon entering the house in deference to the family god. The habit survives in the land "unto this day" as a social grace.

But in my uncle's schoolroom another enterprise went hand in hand with education. Oriental parish priests, of whatever communion, marry, as did the priests of Israel. My uncle had a large family and a small income. Therefore, in order to keep the wolf from the door he betook himself to weaving cloth, on a hand-loom which stood in the schoolroom. The clerical weaver, with flowing hair, luxurious beard, and ample black garb, sat on the edge of the "loom-pit," dug in the floor to accommodate the treadles. He devoted his feet to the treadles, his hands to the shuttle, his eyes to the web, and his ears and tongue to the pupils. At significant moments he would come into living touch with his disciples through a long stick which lay conveniently near his hand.

The only reliable memories I have of my student life in my uncle's school are first, that all the pupils read aloud, at the top of their voices, and thus converted the schoolroom into a veritable beehive. When a mistake happened

to invade the hearing of the teacher he would
shout the name of the transgressing pupil and
acquaint him forcibly with the correct pronun-
ciation. Second, my uncle was infinitely more
interesting to me as a weaver than as an educator. The flitting of the shuttle through the
web entranced me. I watched breathlessly for
the intervals when the sedate cloth-maker
tightened the fabric by turning the heavy
"weaver's beam" over which the finished cloth
was rolled, and to which the writer of First
Samuel likens the staff of Goliath's spear, when
he says, "And the staff of his spear was like a
weaver's beam." It always seemed to me a feat
of strength full of mystery when the arm of the
weaver emerged from his ample, loose sleeve, as
his hand grasped the wooden handle, and made
the giant beam turn with a dull, creaking sound,
and shift the web to the desired position. The
letters of the alphabet, written on a piece of
paper and pasted on the strip of board in my
hand, were nowhere to be compared with the
magical movements of the loom. Therefore,

when my uncle was not looking at me, I was looking at him. That is all.

The second year of my school life found me in more auspicious circumstances. The foreign mission schools were far better equipped than the priests' schools. Therefore, as soon as the English missionaries opened a school in our part of the town, my uncle was compelled to give up his vocation as an educator and devote all his time to his loom and his clerical duties.

The new *Angleez* (English) school held out for me many compelling charms. I was told that there were benches in the schoolroom, a table that had a drawer in it, an iron stove, and a "striking" clock! The teacher built fire *inside* the stove, and a long pipe carried the smoke out of the room. The clock "told" the time. At two o'clock it struck two; at three, three, and so on. The reputation of the teacher was very satisfactory to the parents. He was a severe disciplinarian. "He made the hairs of the pupils' heads stand on end from fear." In a country where the authority of both Church and State inspired fear rather than confidence, this qualification won for the teacher the profound confidence of the people.

At about the age of four I was sent to the *Angleez* school. It was situated in one of the best residences in the town. The schoolroom was large and had two windows. The inventive genius of the English taught the native teacher in charge to put white muslin screens in the windows during the winter season, as substitutes for glass. Each boy had to bring a piece of wood or charcoal every morning to feed the wondrous stove. The clock — a world of mysteries beyond mysteries — told the time. The drawer in the teacher's table seemed an inexhaustible source of dazzling wonders. Fancy pencils, glossy writing-paper, chalks, new, clean little books — all from Beyrout — issued forth from it and enchanted my vision. A large Bible, the first I had seen, rested on the table. There were benches for the older pupils to sit not *on*, but *at*. They sat on the floor and rested their books and elbows on the benches. We, the little ones, had no supports for either our backs, books, or elbows. In a little corner close by the teacher stood an assortment of sticks — light, medium, and extra heavy — which he used with discrimination, according to the ages of the pupils, excepting when in a fit of anger he applied the wrong stick to the right boy. Girls also were permitted to come to the school, but only a few of them attended.

My first and second year in this school carried me through a small primer, a book of Bible stories called "The Bright Light for the Little Boy," a few memory lessons in the Presbyterian catechism, and introduced me to the art of writing. The deepest impression which my teacher made upon me in those days, as a teacher and not as a disciplinarian, was through his conducting of the devotional service which took place at the beginning of every school day. I loved to hear and see him read the Scripture lesson. I felt his prayers reverently. It was inspiring to me to hear his opening sentence; one which he very frequently used was, "O Thou Lord God Almighty, who art over all!" The impression made upon me at those services must have been strong and pleasant, because the whole scene remains with me a clear and delightful memory. I really longed to be like my teacher: to read the Bible with such power and dignity, and to address God in prayer.

That was the first touch of idealism my soul ever felt — the first incentive to aspiration, the first glimpse I had of my higher self as reflected in the strong man who stood before me in the attitude of prayer.

The clearest and most unpleasant memory I have of that teacher, as a disciplinarian, is of a punishment he inflicted upon me which almost proved fatal to both of us. From my present point of view I consider that act to have been most cruel. I do not remember the offense for which my teacher decreed that I be locked up in the schoolroom alone, all night — a child not yet six. The pupils filed out of the room; the teacher, casting a last grim look at me, locked the door and departed. Horrible silence, disturbed only by the now oppressive ticking of the clock, filled the entire building. The shadows began to deepen. My eyes were fastened upon the clock, when an ugly, hairy, black spider sallied forth from some unknown crack, crawled up to the clock, encircled it a few times and retired behind it. I was rigid with fear. I had not enough life to cry. It grew dark; the shadows of death engulfed my soul. Presently I heard steps outside and the voice of my mother. Wondering why I had not come home when it was so late, she had gone out to seek me. Having learned of my plight from the other children, she went to the teacher and asked him to go down to the school without a moment's delay and release me. In what manner she addressed him I was not in a position to know. He instantly obeyed, and I was given my freedom. The next day I fell ill. My father was not at home. My cousins and uncles and second cousins heard of what had happened. Their boy was seriously ill, and the teacher was the

cause. If the boy should die, then *life for life!*
The teacher must die also. So was the teacher
told by one of my uncles who spoke in clear
accents. Poor teacher! Twice a day did he visit
me during that illness, bringing me many presents of things he knew I most longed to have.
His gifts and caresses restored me to health,
and, consequently, assured him of peace and
length of days for himself.

One of my dim but proud memories of the
period under consideration is that of my partici-
pation in a crude miracle play which was
enacted by the children of the Greek Orthodox
faith on what is known in the Greek calendar
as Lazarus Saturday, — the day immediately
preceding Palm Sunday, — in commemoration
of the raising of Lazarus from the dead. That
was our only theatrical performance, whose
setting was the real life of our people which
had undergone no appreciable change since the
time when this miracle was first recorded. We
reproduced the event, as it is reported to have
occurred at that ancient grave in Bethany, at

the door of every adherent of our faith, and were rewarded by the housewife (and woe to her who failed to reward us liberally) with a gift, most often of eggs, which we divided among ourselves at the end of the day and kept for Easter.

The story as reported by the evangelist is written in vernacular poetry on a piece of paper about a foot wide and five feet long. A boy representing Lazarus lies down on the ground and is covered up with a white shroud. Two girls (sometimes boys are substituted, and other changes made in the general plan of procedure), representing Mary and Martha, and dressed in mourning, sit weeping, one at the head, the other at the feet of "Lazarus." Two boys, holding the extended roll over the "corpse," chant with the other boys the poetic tale, until they reach the last line, "Lazarus, Lazarus, arise and speak to me!" — when the brother of Mary and Martha gets up with the "grave-clothes" around him, and turns his sisters' mourning into joy. For many years my sister, who took the rôle of Martha, insisted that when I took the rôle of Lazarus (which was very easy), I should not have known when to "arise" had she not pinched my foot at the psychological moment. For obvious reasons I never admitted her claim.

The last event I remember of my school career in El-Shweir was the coming of the English missionary — the *khawaja* himself — to inspect our school. This was a gala day. The *khawaja* was to give prizes to deserving pupils. My teacher, partly because I was a "bright boy" and partly because of my recent illness, which he was supposed to have caused, had taught me the Beatitudes by heart, that I might repeat them on that occasion and perchance get a prize. The *khawaja* was the first man I had seen dressed in *effrenjee* (European costume). The native dress for men was the *shirwal* (ample bloomers), and the man in pantaloons was a great curiosity. I repeated the Beatitudes in the august presence of the *khawaja* and many of the parents and the

LAZARUS MIRACLE-PLAY

school, and to my unspeakable delight received
a pen-knife for a prize.

About this time, when I was six years old,
my parents decided to move from El-Shweir to
a town called Betater, situated about thirty
miles to the south on the western slopes of
Mount Lebanon. My father had been in charge
for some years of all the building operations
of a Frenchman who had a large silk-spinning
factory in that town, and it was natural for
him to desire to have his family with him.

To depart from one's kindred in Syria has
always been a painful operation, from the time
of the patriarch Abraham. The thought of
being buried "in the land of strangeness" is to
a Syrian especially hard to bear. But if the
sepulchre of our fathers was not in Betater, our
church — the Greek Orthodox — was there to
give us spiritual kinsmen, and to give our
bodies burial in its consecrated ground.

On a bright spring morning, late in April, I
was awakened from sleep at early dawn. Com-

ing out to the yard, I saw three mules and a donkey standing on the east side of the house. Two of the mules were heavily laden with our clothes-chests, bedding, and other movable furniture. The third mule was made ready for my mother and my baby sister to ride on, and the donkey was likewise fitted for my sister, next older, and my brother, next younger than myself, and me.

Was it possible that I was to have such a long donkey-ride? The very earth under my feet vibrated with joy. It was not at all painful to leave one's kindred if by so doing one might have such a ride!

Neighbors and friends stood around weeping and lamenting our departure. My mother, with streaming eyes, assured them that our sojourn in the "strange country" would be short, and that by Allah's [1] will our return to our kindred was assured. Presently our neigh-

---

[1] Allah, the familiar designation for the Deity in the Arabic language, is used by Christians as well as by Mohammedans.

bor's wife, casting a bewildered look skyward above the oak trees, crossed herself and in solemn accents said, "God cast thee off, you evil presence! Off at the beginning of this momentous day!" She spat in the direction of the evil object; so did all those present, making the sign of the cross. It was a crow! The black navigator of the air was very gay on that spring morning, regardless of all solemn abjuration and vigorous spitting. But he was, nevertheless, a decidedly evil omen at the beginning of a journey. This had been proved a thousand times. Presently one of the men said, "I see another!" "*Kheir, kheir!*" (good, good!) exclaimed the others. The crows, when traveling in pairs, brought no evil on those who saw them. They neutralized each other.

During all that time, however, my eyes were fixed on the donkey. His charms were enough to neutralize the evil of a thousand and one crows. Every movement of his ears carved a line in my heart. Life certainly became worth the living when my cousin turned around and said, "Abraham, come; come on the donkey's back." I do not believe I weighed more than ten ounces when I was being transferred from the ground to the cushioned back of the donkey. I floated in the ether. Amidst sobs and tears and *"Ma'essalamy"* (go in safety), "Allah be with you," "May no evil touch you," "Send back good news with the muleteer," and so forth, the muleteer, after invoking the Holy Name, called, *"Dah, dah!"* The mules, tossing their heads in the air, proceeded on their way; so did my donkey, to whose back I was tied with a rope to keep me from falling when he went up and down hills.

Up the steep hill proceeded our little caravan, reaching the crest just as the sun began to gild "the high pinnacles of the earth." The two muleteers and two of our cousins — strong and valiant men — formed our escort. The picture of my sad mother on that morning as she sat on the mule's back, the right end of her *mendeel* (long bead scarf) turned under her chin and thrown over the left shoulder, my baby sister in her lap, and one of my cousins walking by her side, stands in my memory as the original of "The Flight to Egypt."

Miles of pine trees stretched along our way. Rough, rocky roads followed the slopes of the hills, dipping into deep valleys and climbing again to high summits. The world appeared to me delightfully new and immeasurably large. The deep blue haze of the distant mountains seemed like the border-line of another world. Now and then we met a nobleman in richly embroidered attire, mounted on a lavishly decorated horse, with his sword dangling at his side and his footmen pacing reverently before him.

Twice we halted on our way by springs of water "to sustain our hearts with food." My childish eyes never beheld a more delightful sight than that of the "bread bundles" — thin loaves folded together like napkins, three or four in a bundle — as they were pulled by the muleteer out of the saddlebag filled with the delicacies which are usually provided for such occasions in Syria. One bundle contained ripe olives sprinkled with pulverized thyme, another, small cakes of cheese dipped in olive oil, another, figs "cooked" in grape molasses, another, boiled eggs, etc. We arrived at our destination about dusk. The rope with which I had been tied to the donkey's back had entered into such intimate relations with my legs that when I dismounted I found them utterly unavailable for use. I was carried into the house, most deservedly. The half of a double house, into which our family was ushered upon our arrival at Betater, consisted of three rooms, — a lower room where we lived during the winter season, an upper room where we lived the rest of the year, and a rear storeroom.

Betater was inhabited by Christians and Druses, who were in the majority and the ruling class, and some Mohammedans. The Christians represented the Greek Orthodox, Greek Catholic, and Maronite churches. As usual, they lived at war with one another and united as "Christians" only when attacked by the

THE RIHBANY HOME AT BETATER

The right half of a double house

Druses. The clannish feuds also existed within the various sects. We, however, were "strangers," and, having no clan of our own in the town, were immune from attacks by any and all of the clans because of our weakness. "Thou shalt not oppress a stranger" is a command which is universally observed in Syria. However, we were free to side with our fellow Greek Orthodox, as they were expected to defend us. My father, however, would participate in no fight. But in Betater we had a clan of Druse Sheikhs who were the noblemen and rulers of the community. The common people "belonged" to the Sheikhs. Each Sheikh was the "lord protector" of a certain number of families. As in El-Shweir we had no aristocracy of any kind, it was very strange to me that our family should "belong" to a superior personage.

My father was known in the community as the "Master" (builder). Our family was designated as the "Master's family," and I was addressed as "Abraham, the Master's son," just as Joshua had been known as "the son of Nun." We were often called "Shweiriah," from our birthplace, and in accordance with the ancient Syrian custom, as, "David, son of Jesse, the Bethlehemite." The Sheikhs were to me a new human species. Their costly garments of choice Oriental fabrics, their richly inlaid swords and thoroughbred Arabian horses, were the visions of a new world for me.

I was carefully taught the etiquette of life among such dignitaries. When saluting a Sheikh I was to kiss his hand and call him "My Lord." I was not to engage in conversation in the presence of a Sheikh without first having his permission. Coming into an assembly where a Sheikh was, I could not sit down until he had commanded me to do so. To these and other social graces I applied myself diligently.

It was among those Sheikhs that I first heard men swear by their heads. Swearing by one's head is an ancient Oriental custom, peculiar to aristocrats and inappropriately imitated at times by the common people. It always betrays such arrogance and haughtiness as to show why Jesus said, "Neither shalt thou swear by thy head, because thou canst not make one hair white or black." There also I first arrived at the realization that the priest was holier than myself; the Sheikh nobler. Why? It was a holy mystery. The priest explained it to me a few times thus: The Gospel said, "Let every soul be subject unto the higher powers — the powers that be are ordained of God." So the priests and aristocrats were those "higher powers." The explanation always seemed to me to be simple, authoritative, and fully satisfactory.

My memories of our first few years' residence in Betater are most delightful. The inhabitants, Christians and Druses, aristocrats and commoners, rivaled one another in doing us favors. They were bound that the *ghareeb* (stranger) should feel perfectly at home in their midst. When the fruit and vegetable season came, seeing that we had no vineyards of our own, our new neighbors poured in upon us a veritable deluge of baskets of such products of the soil. In our first and second year in the "land of strangeness" so many baskets of the golden grapes of Lebanon were sent to us that we made our whole year's supply of raisins, wine, and vinegar.

I shall never forget that awe-inspiring manifestation of sympathy for us by the people of Betater when my five-year-old brother died. Because we had no relatives in the town "to comfort us," and notwithstanding the fact that the deceased was only a child, his funeral equaled in dignity that of an influential citizen. The "comforters" who came to us seemed to me a multitude which no man could number. Although according to custom only a few of the young Sheikhs represent the noble clan at such a funeral, in this case nearly the entire clan attended. They came up to our house with their attendants of the Druse commoners, in what seemed to my childish mind an endless line of white turbans, long beards, Damascus gowns, and Persian cloaks. With characteristic dignity and tender Oriental effusiveness they assured my sorrowing father that his affliction was theirs also; that he should not consider himself a stranger in their midst, because they thought of him as one of them; and that their homes and all they possessed were at his disposal.

My first visit to the great city of Beyrout was an epoch-maker. I was not yet quite nine when my father yielded to my long-continued pleading with him to take me to the far-famed metropolis. As the common people of Syria rarely could indulge in the luxury of having *merkûbs* (mounts) in traveling, I was expected to walk all the way, a distance of about fifteen miles. I use the word "miles" here in accordance with the Western custom. In my native land we measured distance by different means. An object or a place was as far as a "stone's throw," or the "smoking of a cigarette," — as the Syrians inhale the tobacco smoke deeply, the literal expression is the "drinking of a cigarette," — or an hour's, two hours', or a

day's journey, as the case might be. Of course
I agreed to walk to Beyrout with most solemn
affirmations. My father, a cousin of ours, and
I proceeded one day down the stony footpaths
on the western slopes of Mount Lebanon toward
the ancient city. My little legs remained firm
until we were about halfway on our journey
when my steps began to falter. The gentlemen
of the party threatened to leave me behind,
and feigned that they would continue on their
way without me. Their scheme, however,
failed of its purpose; I could not be aroused to
further exertion. I simply cried, howled, and
implored my teasers. Then, I assure you, there
was no leaving me behind. First, Cousin
Suleiman carried me on his back "a lift," then
father came second with another lift, and so on,
until we reached the crowded, crooked streets
of Beyrout; then I was ready again to walk.

But the fatigue of the journey did not prevent my father and Cousin Suleiman from giving me most earnestly and solemnly detailed
instructions as to how I should conduct myself

while in Beyrout. I was not to gaze curiously at the Mohammedans, whom I knew by their white turbans. They considered us *kûffar* (infidels) and enemies of the faith; therefore they were ever ready for the slightest provocation to beat or even kill us. In the presence of a Mohammedan I was to assume a most reverential and humble attitude.

Again, I was not to stray away from my guardians, — not even a few yards, — because the cursed Jews might steal me and murder me. I was told that the sons of Abraham feasted on the blood of Christian children. Several instances were mentioned to me when Christian children, known to my kindred, had been captured in the Jewish quarter in Beyrout and bled to death by those enemies of Christ. My flesh crept and crawled when the process of "bleeding" was described to me. The Christian child was led into a chamber within seven doors. He was stripped naked, placed in a cradle lined with sharp darning-needles and rocked violently until every drop of blood in him had been drawn; the blood was then sealed in bottles and preserved for the *fûsseh* (the feast of the Passover). How my people secured this accurate knowledge of Jewish cruelty, how they unlocked the secrets of those chambers of horror which existed "within seven doors," and from whose bourne, according to their own statements, no traveler ever returned, neither I nor any other Syrian Christian ever thought of asking.

Amidst such apprehensions and fears I spent two days in Beyrout on that first visit. The city seemed endless in extent and alive with mysteries. There I stood for the first time on the seashore and watched the restless waters with worshipful awe; there I first learned objectively what the word "carriage" meant, saw a few kerosene street lamps, ate all the *balaway* (a Syrian sweet dear to children) I wanted to eat, and bought a little harmonica, the only musical instrument that our family ever possessed.

In the absence of a foreign school in Betater

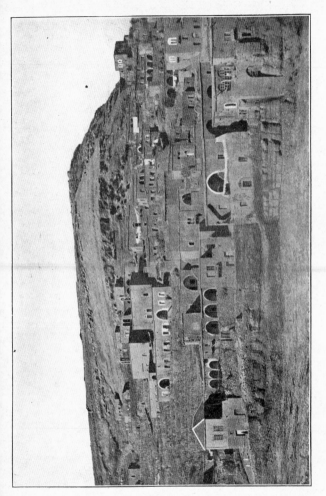

BETATER

AT THE FEET OF MY TEACHERS

I resumed my studies under the Maronite priest. Our own priest kept no school. But my mother disliked the Maronites very much. Her reason for this was that they did not baptize in the right way; that in making the sign of the cross they touched the left shoulder before the right, and were the slaves of the Pope of Rome who shaved all his face.[1] Therefore when, the second year after our arrival in Betater, an American mission school was opened in the town, I was immediately transferred to it.

Both Protestants and Maronites were in error, but the Protestants were better teachers. In this school I stayed two years. I read a

[1] The reader must remember that the Maronite priests who are subject to Rome cut the hair of their heads, but not their beards, but the Greek Orthodox pride themselves on the fact that, after consecration, their priests never shave or cut the hair of their heads, thus conforming strictly to the law of the "Nazarite," or as Scripture has it, "separated unto God." Thus when Hannah, the mother of Samuel, asked a "man child" of the Lord she vowed, saying, "Then I will give him unto the Lord all the days of his life, and there shall no razor come upon his head." 1 Sam. 1, 11. See also Num. VI, 5.

large part of the Bible, advanced in arithmetic
up to "long division," had a few lessons in
geography, and was supposed to have become
efficient enough to write a letter. This, however, I always dreaded when called upon to do
it by my father. It was not the business part
of the letter which I dreaded, because that was
dictated to me; but I had to write the "preface,"
a chapter of fulsome salaams and laudatory
phrases, extolling the recipient, without which
a letter was little short of an insult. Again, I
had to ascertain "the day of the month" which,
in the entire absence of calendars, was known
only to a few select minds. When the question,
"How much of the month is it?" was put to
me, my face reddened with incredible swiftness.
And when I was ridiculed by the men present
for my inexcusable ignorance, being a "schoolboy," my mother would come to the rescue by
telling those men that they themselves did not
know how much of the month it was, and they
were of much larger dimensions than I was. I
was often sent to the priest to ask him what day

of the month it was. He usually counted on his fingers from the last saint's day, according to the Eastern calendar, and I ran home with the information lest I should forget it on the way.

When I was nine years old, it happened one day that my teacher punished me rather severely. I grabbed my books and ran to where my father was working, crying bitterly. Of course I told my father that the teacher was absolutely merciless. He seemed very much distressed and concluded that I had had enough schooling anyway, and that it was time that I exchanged books for tools and began learning my father's trade. It was so ordered, and at the age of nine I began my career as a stone-mason.

CHAPTER IV

THE RELIGION OF MY FATHERS

LET now the story of my industrial evolution bide its time. The story of my earliest religious faith and life should have precedence.

In the absence of anything to the contrary, I have reason to assume that my first Christian ancestors were among the converts of Paul and Barnabas in the ancient see of Antioch, and that a Christian ancestry spanning nineteen centuries lies behind me. Within the fold of the ancient Greek Orthodox Church I first learned to lisp the names of God, Christ, the Church, and the Gospel. Mary, the "Mother of God," and a host of saints also claimed my affectionate reverence. I was taught by my parents, more by example than precept, and most conscientiously, to observe the ordinances of my church.

And here I wish to speak of the church of my fathers and my childhood and youth, not according to my present knowledge of it as a student of church history, but as I knew it as a common worshiper, and as it is known to the large majority of its adherents all over the world.[1]

To go to mass and to believe that my church was the one and only true church were my first lessons in the faith. For private devotion I was taught three prayers, the Lord's Prayer, the Apostles' Creed, and "Hail Mary." I was instructed by both example and precept to observe the fasts—the Great Lent, which precedes Easter, lasts fifty days; the Fast of the Nativity, forty days; the Fast of the Apostles, generally forty days; the Fast of the Virgin, fifteen days; and every Wednesday and Friday. During all these fasts the faithful are expected to abstain from such foods as meat, eggs, milk, cheese, and, during the Great Lent and the Fast of the Virgin, fish, excepting on two occasions. To make an honest confession, the fasts were most oppressive to me. During Lent I was expected to taste no food until noon. I was willing to abstain from meat foods, but the

[1] See Appendix.

òccasions when I did really fast until noon were extremely rare. So long as I could obtain food, by either fair or foul means, I broke the fast early in the day, on the theory that devouring hunger was a greater imperative than any church ordinance.

No pews are allowed in the Eastern churches. The people stand with folded arms during the entire service. Two small groups of readers or singers, one to the right, the other to the left of the altar, assist the priest at the mass. When at church I always stood by the reading-desk, where I had a good view of the priest. At one time I was accorded the honor of reading the Epistle, which preceded the reading of the Gospel at the mass. I could not have been much more than eight years old at the time. One of the good old men taught me for about two weeks how to intone the Apostolic lines. The Epistle was from St. Paul and began with the word, "Brethren." When the solemn moment arrived, I was beckoned to stand before the *anastasis* (a partition which screens the altar from the congregation) immediately in front of the Royal Gate, through which only the priest is permitted to pass. My normal consciousness lasted until I reached the appointed spot and uttered the word, "Brethren." Then all was darkness. I could hear a hollow, sepulchral voice issuing from somewhere. I woke up again by the reader's desk. My father reached down and kissed me. The singer put his hand on my head and whispered, "Bright boy!" That restored my soul.

An event which occurred about this time and which burned itself deeply into my memory, was a fight which took place in church during mass. It is the custom in the Greek Church for a layman to lead the congregation in the Lord's Prayer and the Apostles' Creed. An elderly man of a certain clan had been in the habit of leading in the Lord's Prayer for years. Certain men of another clan thought that old Sallume had enjoyed that honor long enough and concluded to wrest it from him. On one Sunday morning, as Sallume began to repeat the Lord's

Prayer, a man of the opposing clan began to repeat the same at the reading-desk on the left.

Sallume was greatly exasperated. Addressing both the Almighty and his saucy opponent, Sallume's wrathful version of the Prayer was thus: "Our Father"—("Hush up, you wretch")—"Hallowed be"—("It is my heritage from my fathers, you dog")—"thy name." ("I will tread on your neck"—"Curse your entire clan," and so on). The other man was no milder in his devotional language, and they met in combat in front of the Royal Gate. The men of their respective clans rushed forward from all parts of the church, and the fight became general. It was at that point of the mass when the priest was repeating what are called "the mystic words," and, according to his holy orders, he could not look back upon the congregation, even though the church were deluged with blood. But soon after he was done with the mystic rite, he pulled off his sacred robes from him, grabbed a heavy staff,[1] and

[1] In the absence of seats in the Greek churches, long

cleared the church. The fighting continued outside the building until the Turkish soldiers arrived.

The most impressive part of the Greek Orthodox service (aside from the great festivals), which I still remember with grateful appreciation, was the administering of the "holy *korban*" (sacrament of the Lord's Supper) to a communicant during mass. The scene never failed to thrill me through and through with religious emotion.

The humble applicant for the adorable sacramental elements, who has previously confessed his sins to the priest, with his head bowed and his arms folded on his breast, comes forward and stands immediately in front of the Royal Gate. He lifts his eyes slightly toward the impressively silent congregation and says, "Forgive me, O Christians, whatever transgressions I may have committed against you!" — which petition the congregation answer in

T-shaped staves are provided for elderly men, on which they lean forward during mass.

scarcely audible accents, "May God forgive you!" Then, as the priest appears through the Royal Gate with the sacred cup, the applicant turns and faces the altar, reaches for the silk napkin hanging from the priest's hand, and holds it under his chin, to guard against the possibility of any part of the consecrated elements dropping onto the floor; and, as the priest lifts the golden spoon out of the cup with its precious contents of bread and wine, and conveys it to the lips of the penitent son of the Church, the singers chant alternately and most impressively the solemn words: "Accept me this day as partaker of thy mystic supper, O Son of God, for I will not betray thy secret to thine enemies, nor give thee a kiss as Judas did, but like the thief cry to thee, Remember me, O Lord, when thou comest into thy kingdom."

Many years have elapsed since my eyes last beheld such a scene; I have given up belief in the dogma of transubstantiation and the authority of the confessional; nevertheless, the religious *feelings* I experienced in my early

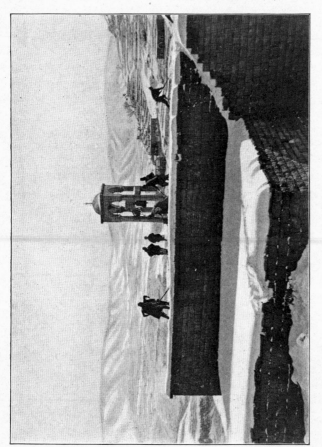

SHOVELING SNOW OFF THE CHURCH ROOF

years on such occasions remain with me, precious spiritual realities.

The feasts and festivals of the Greek Church filled my boyish heart with delight, so spectacular and so full of mystery were they. The Syrian churches do not make much of Christmas because originally it was not an Oriental holiday. New Year's, or "Good-Morning Day," as the Syrians call it, was the day when we exchanged presents and indulged in much gayety. But what was of absorbing interest to me as a boy, aside from the few coppers and sugar-plums that I got for presents, was the offering I carried to the fountain, early on New Year's morning. My older sisters went with their jars to carry water for the household, and I went with them. We took with us a few handfuls of wheat and cereals and cast them reverently into the water, saying "Good-morning, fountain! Bless and increase our grain!" So did we ignorantly practice the modes of worship of our remote Oriental ancestors, who poured their gifts to Astarte into the streams

of Syria ages before Christianity was born.
And who are you, child of but yesterday, to say
it was all empty superstition?

But what was all that compared to the feast
of Epiphany, which we celebrated in commemoration of the baptism of Jesus in the river
Jordan, twelve days after Christmas? It is
known to the people as *El-Gitas* (dipping in
water). I was taught to believe, and most joy-
ously did believe, that the rivers and fountains
of the entire world became suddenly holy about
sunset on the eve of Epiphany. Wild beasts
left not their dens the entire night, and were all
rendered harmless as doves, because the Christ
was on his way to the Jordan. The trees
"knelt" before the passing Saviour, with the
exception of the mulberry and the fig, which
saucily remained standing. It was explained to
me in this connection that the mulberry tree
was too proud to kneel because it produced
silk, and the fig tree had a grudge against the
Master because he once cursed it. And how
I would go out on that blessed night and peer

into the darkness to see a "kneeling" tree! But I was always told that only a saint could see such things.

But my failure to see a "kneeling" tree always awakened my greater curiosity to know whether any saint then living ever did really behold such a sight. I was told that only one godly man (who, unfortunately, had been dead for many years) of our own clan did see a "kneeling" tree, under peculiarly interesting circumstances. The custom is that on the blessed night of Epiphany many men go to the streams of water, preferably about midnight, and "baptize" themselves with Christ. It was at such a time that the devout Abu-Simaan besought a creek which ran near our town to secure a closer fellowship with the Saviour through the commemorative act. He removed his garments and instinctively placed them on the dry limbs of a fallen tree close by the stream, instead of on the wet ground, and plunged into the water. Emerging from the water he was amazed to find that both the tree and his belongings were gone. Greatly bewildered, he looked hither and thither, until he saw his clothes in the top of a lofty poplar tree, some distance away. With great joy Abu-Simaan quickly realized that when he threw his garments over its branches the tree was kneeling! That he had had the rare fortune to be "baptized" just at the most blessed moment when the Christ was walking the earth in the mystic shadows which veiled Him from mortal eyes. The devout Abu-Simaan crossed himself repeatedly, said his prayer, and then climbed the tree and regained his belongings. But whenever I heard that enchanting story what forced itself upon my little mind, and almost spoiled the miracle for me, was the significant question, "How did poor old Abu-Simaan manage, especially in his Adamic state, to climb to the top of such a tall tree?"

The material feast of Epiphany was *zulabiah* (fried cakes of the doughnut variety). I do not remember that I ever was unwilling to do any errand for my mother which served to further the cause of "frying" on that sacred occasion. The *zulabiah* must be fried in pure olive oil over a fire of olive wood, whenever it could be obtained, for the olive is the most sacred among the trees. It was supreme joy to me to feed the fire while my mother fried the cakes, to see the bars, coils, and balls of dough swell and sizzle in the hot oil, and to watch my mother take them out of the frying-pan, brown and hissing, and drop them into a large basin of grape molasses. A choice quantity of *zulabiah* we gave to the priest, when he came with his attendant on Epiphany day and sprinkled holy water at the door and in the four corners of the house, with an olive branch tied to a small cross.

"Baptizing" the sacred yeast was a delight to me. At every baking the Syrian housewife saves out a small lump of dough for a "leaven" for the next baking. But at the last baking before Epiphany no leaven is saved. A new leaven, miraculously raised at this time, provided the yeast for the coming year. My mother would mix a small quantity of dough, just in cold water, and no yeast whatever, tie it up in a piece of white cloth and give it to me to hang up in a tree that "knelt." For three mornings I carried the yeast to the fountain, immersed it three times, in the name of the Father, Son, and Holy Ghost, repeating the chant of my Church: "By Thy baptism, O Lord, in the river Jordan was made clear the adoration of the Holy Trinity. The voice of the Father witnessed to Thee, calling Thee the beloved Son. And the Spirit in the form of a dove also witnessed to Thee. O Thou who hast appeared and enlightened the world, Thou Christ-God, glory be to Thee!"

The yeast hung in the tree for three days, then was taken into the house, and behold a miracle! The dough was raised without yeast! Did not my remote un-Christian ancestors so manifest their devotion when their sacred trees hung with votive gifts?

The Easter festival stands greatest among the festivals of the Greek church. Our priest

THE PRIEST SPRINKLING HOLY WATER
ON EPIPHANY DAY

often said that the picture of the Virgin looked very sad on Good Friday and smiled on Easter.

The Great Lent was to us a period of self-denial and religious contemplation and prayer. I would not say that we were always burning with zeal during this long period for the things of the spirit. We did, however, pray more during Lent than at any other time. I repeated my three prayers mentioned above, every night, and knelt[1] and kissed the ground (a sign of humility before God) from three to six times, while I repeated these words: "O God of power, be thou with us; for in times of sorrow we have no helper but thee; O God of power, be with us."

But the somber hue of those days of self-denial began to grow lighter and more cheery for me when my mother commenced, about the middle of the lenten season, to make my holiday clothes. I was not "fitted" for the occasion at a department store; in those days we

[1] Kneeling in prayer is not required by the Greek Church except during Lent.

never even so much as heard of such an establishment. The dry-goods peddler came to our house, and out of his well-stocked pack brought forth fabrics of dazzling colors and designs. The cloth for my holiday attire was never "cut" either on a Tuesday or in the "waning of the moon." Garments cut on such unauspicious occasions brought evil upon their wearer. No pattern was needed; I myself was there and the suit was fashioned after my own mortal frame. To watch every stitch, and to try the garments on at frequent intervals, provided me with a protracted entertainment, with a series of sensations which made my passage through the sober days of Lent to the Easter festival not only tolerable, but extremely interesting. On Good Friday I flew over the hills to gather wild flowers with which the cross was covered in a little coffin, in commemoration of the burial of Jesus. Saturday was spent in gathering roots and vegetables with which we colored the multitude of Easter eggs. On the night of that day I went to bed with my holiday clothes on, in order not to lose the precious moments of the morning in dressing, after the church bell had called the faithful to the sanctuary. Soon after midnight, on Saturday, the church bell pealed the glorious message of the Resurrection. I woke with the words, "Christ is risen!" on my lips. "Of a truth he is risen!" was the answer. I kissed my parents' hands, and we all proceeded to the church to enjoy the glorious Easter ritual.

The supreme moment for me during the Easter mass came when the "charge" was made, symbolizing the victory of Christ over Satan. The entire congregation, following the priest, marched three times around the church, each carrying a lighted taper. Then all marched out of the church, only one man, who represented Satan, remaining inside. He closed the church door and stood close behind it, to prevent the risen Lord from entering into heaven. I never can think of that "multitude that kept holy-day," of their many-colored garments, of the ringing voice of the priest, and of the host of lighted tapers which converted the assembly into a mass of flame, without thinking of the words of Isaiah, "Ye shall have a song, as in the night when a holy solemnity is kept!"

The priest who represented Christ approached the door with the multitude behind him and in a most solemn voice chanted the words of the psalmist: "Lift up your heads, O ye gates, and be ye lifted up, ye everlasting doors, and the King of Glory shall come in!" The man inside said in a sneering tone, "Who is this King of Glory?" "The Lord of Hosts," said the priest, "he is the King of Glory!" Thrice was the chant repeated; then the hindering Satan, vanquished, barked like a dog, and the priest forced the door open and marched in with the multitude, chanting, "Let God arise and let his enemies be scattered!"

In those days my mother Church was all-sufficient for me. The so-called "period of storm and stress" in religion is unknown to sacramental worship. I was born into my faith; and my faith was ready-made for me. The confessional, fasts, and sacraments of the Church met my every need. Reasoning about religion was never known to my forefathers, and I was not supposed to go so far as to indulge in it. But I did, and that early in my youth. Early in my youth I felt the inward urgency to reason, not only *within* the tenets of my faith, but *about* and *beyond* them. But the atmosphere of my early life was not favorable to such modes of thinking. Therefore, my battling with the issues of religion had to be postponed to a later time.

CHAPTER V

WHEN I was taken out of school at the age of nine and introduced to manual labor, my father deemed it wise to have me begin my industrial career under other auspices than his own. The French silk-spinner, M. Fortune Portalis, of whose building enterprises my father had sole charge, employed a large number of boys and girls in his factory, where the work was supposed to be less arduous than that which the building operations required. The great Frenchman was known to us as "Fertoni" — an Arabianized form of his given name. He was a tyrant, a hero, a heartless employer, a philanthropist, a physician, a shrewd business man, an infidel, and a churchman, all in one. For me he was the supreme wonder of the mundane order. The Turkish Government — always cruel to her own subjects, but helpless in dealing with foreigners — had no control over Fer-

[104]

toni whatever. In dealing with his employees he was himself the employer, the judge, and the jury; he would either bribe them with money or coerce them with the whip, just as it suited him. The inhabitants of the region for miles around his factory, both aristocrats and commoners, contemplated him with profound awe.

Upon our arrival in Betater the wonders which were in store for me to see were Fertoni and his *kirkhana* (factory). The *kirkhana* had a gable roof covered with zinc; it contained wheels, water-pipes, a furnace, and a boiler — things which my eyes never had seen before. And what was still more enchanting than all these was the fact that Fertoni's bedroom was lined with pictures — wall-paper which was utterly unknown to us. And, oh, how I would come to the window of that bedroom, when the dread Fertoni was nowhere to be seen, and gaze upon those decorated walls as upon the bewitching scenes of paradise! The bedstead and the fringed counterpane, also, enhanced in my mind the greatness of France.

A FAR JOURNEY

The first duty to which I addressed myself as an industrial worker at Fertoni's *kirkhana* was the picking up of silk cocoons from under the many-storied drying-tables, on which the precious cocoons were spread and turned over twice a day by men who were called "turners," in order to dry speedily and evenly. My wage was two pennies per day, and the hours of labor from dawn until dusk.

I do not remember that following the "turners" and picking up cocoons was in itself a very hard task, but when I think of the foreman who ruled over us in those days, the month I spent under him as a cocoon-picker rises in my mind as a harrowing memory. Dawood, son of Suleiman, was perhaps the meanest man Fertoni ever honored with the office of a foreman. I never saw that man smile. He stands before me now in the form of a man of medium size, his face pale, his lips thin and firm, his features rigid and ungenerous, his speech harsh and profane, and very often reinforced with the cruel use of a slender, tough stick which never left his hand during business hours. Fertoni himself was a tyrant, but his tyranny had somewhat of the heroic in it, which often made it an object of admiration. But Dawood was an arrogant coward, and my fear of him was thoroughly saturated with hatred and contempt. All the men hated him, but could not chastise him because back of him was Fertoni, and back of Fertoni, France. I bore the yoke of the petty tyrant for a month, and if I were to live my life over again I should implore the Almighty to blot out that month from the calendar of my years. My father's object in having me begin my industrial career under the authority of strangers was to give me a sort of discipline which he thought I would not get under him. But my mother thought that a month's work under the hated Dawood was discipline enough for any one; therefore at her urging I was taken out of the silk factory at the end of the month and put to work with my father as an apprentice to the stone-mason trade.

At that time my father was at the height of his prosperity. He employed from thirty to fifty men, and was sought from far and near as a builder. The men under his control were classified on religious lines, following the Syrian custom from time immemorial. They numbered so many Druses, so many Greek Orthodox, so many Maronites, and so forth. The common laborer received five piastres (twenty cents) a day, and the master mason from twelve to fifteen piastres. My social environment as an industrial worker afforded no strong incentives to progress. From the days of the Pyramids and the Hanging Gardens of Babylon to this day no spark has ever disturbed the clod of the laboring masses of the East. Their lot gave no play to the imagination. They knew no common interest, no collective action, no citizenship, no political rights. Their day's work began at dawn and ended at dusk. The moral atmosphere I breathed among those men did not really blossom with lofty ideals. Owing to the complete segregation of the sexes in the

Orient and the absence of education, male society is by no means "holy in all manner of conversation."

One of the never-to-be-forgotten phenomena of my early years, a spectacle which the most extravagantly imaginative American mind cannot picture, was the coming of the locusts into our part of the country. If my memory serves me well, I was about twelve years old when my father and all his men, together with all the male population over fifteen, were impressed by the governor of our district to fight the devastating hosts of Oriental locusts. No one who has not seen such a spectacle and the desolation those winged creatures leave behind them can appreciate in the least degree the force of the saying of "the Lord God of the Hebrews" to Pharaoh, "If thou refuse to let my people go, behold, to-morrow I will bring the locusts into thy coasts." For a few weeks before they deluged our district the news came with the caravans that the locusts were sweeping toward our region from the "land of the south." We youngsters did not know why our elders were so terror-stricken when they heard of it, until the scourge had come and gone.

It was a few weeks before the time of the harvest when the clouds of locusts enveloped our community. They hid the sun with their greenish-yellow wings, covered the trees and the ground, the walls and roofs of the houses, and dashed in our faces like flakes of snow driven by the wind. The utter hopelessness of the task which confronted our people and seemed to unite all classes in despair, assumed in my sight a very comic aspect, and converted the calamity into a holiday. It was so amusing to me to see our sedate aristocrats and old men and women join the youth and common laborers in shouting, beating on tin cans, firing muskets, setting brush on fire, striking at the cursed insects with their hands, stamping them with their feet, and praying God to send "a strong wind" to drive the enemy of man away. Every *mutekellif* (payer of the toll-tax) had to fight the locusts for so many days or hire a substitute.

A STONE-MASON

I do not clearly remember whether it was the beating on tin cans and howling of the people or the prayed-for "strong wind" that drove the merry locusts away. What I do remember is that when they did go away they left the land almost stripped clean of every green thing. It was no vain threatening when the writer of Deuteronomy warned Israel, saying, "If thou wilt not hearken unto the voice of the Lord thy God, to observe to do all his commandments . . . All thy trees and fruit of thy land shall the locust consume."

Of the hardships of my environment I had my full share as a boy. The entire lack of machinery doubled the hardships of our work. The long hours of labor and the bad sanitation were a constant menace to both the soul and the body. When our work took us away from our home town, we generally traveled by night, "to save time" and to escape the heat of the day. Sometimes we would travel all night, afoot, carrying our tools and other belongings on our backs. As the Master's son I was often relieved of carrying tools by the men, but it was hard enough for a tender youth to undergo even the ordinary hardships of such a life.

But my industrial career had a brighter side. As the Master's son I enjoyed privileges which seldom fall to an apprentice. I was second in command over the men, after my father, and for that reason they accorded me the respect which my years did not really merit. The master masons under my father gave me every advantage to learn the trade. At the early age of fourteen I was allowed to "mount the wall," — to do actual building, — and, at the age of sixteen, I was classed and paid wages as a "master." I was very thorough, very conscientious in my work, and was, therefore, in great demand. My father was very much pleased with my progress and had no doubt but that I would continue the traditions of the family as a stone-mason. But the mysteries of life are so deep and so numerous that, even in a static society such as that into which I was born, no

SUPPORTING A STONE CARRIER

one could tell which direction the current of destiny might take.

Already at the age of fourteen I had become mysteriously discontented with my lot. I had begun to dream, in a very vague way, to be sure, of better things. I distinctly remember that the thought of being a stone-mason all my life oppressed me at that early age. "Am I to be only a toiler all my life?" was a question which often pressed in my mind for an answer. Life under such conditions seemed to me to possess no permanent significance. My restlessness greatly disturbed my father. To him it was the result of pride and vanity, and nothing else.

It was about this time, I believe, that I first heard of America. The news of that remote and strange country came to me simply as a bit of indifferent knowledge. Some Syrians had gone to America and returned with much money. Money in America was of very little value. But the country was so far away, so difficult of access, that those who reached it must have done so by accident. The American missionaries were known to us as English.

But at the age of fourteen something of much greater significance came into my life. I made the acquaintance of a boy of about my age who was attending an American boarding-school, about ten miles away from our town. Iskander was the only boy of our town who had ever been sent to such a school, and was therefore very conspicuous in the community for his dignity and "learning."

How I became acquainted with Iskander and how he allowed himself to become the most intimate friend of such a boy as I was, I cannot tell. It was simply destiny. Iskander was a fine penman. He knew much poetry, arithmetic, geography, and English, many things about the Bible, and many other mysteries. He knew a great deal about America, and much about other countries. When he came home for his summer vacation of three months, we practically lived together. Iskander would read poetry to me and teach me words in the classical

Arabic. Our conversations covered every phase of thought in which he was interested, and brought me treasures of knowledge. Not infrequently we would stay up the whole night, engaged in such conversations. Here certainly a revolution came into my life. I loved knowledge and craved more of its higher pleasures. Of a truth, as it seemed to me, I was never made to be an ignorant toiler. I was an idealist. But such a life as that of my friend Iskander seemed far beyond me. I never could hope to become so learned as he, and never had the remotest idea of going to school.

My father was glad that the "learned" Iskander was my friend, but he had no patience with "the frills of poetry" for a stone-mason. "There is no bread in the foolishness of poetry; tools, tools only can feed our hunger," was one of his answers to my pretentious remarks. My good father was right, inasmuch as he knew only of one hunger to feed. At the age of sixteen I became decidedly averse to working at the mason's trade. My discontent began to beget wickedness in my mind. In the absence of my friend Iskander, at school, I fell into the company of certain idlers who were no more nor less than highway robbers. The stories of their adventures greatly fascinated me, and I was in great danger of taking the wrong course in life. My parents were greatly alarmed at this, and strained every effort to ease my difficulties and lead me in the way in which I should go. But the pitiable fact was that neither they nor I had any definite object in view. It was discontent on my part and anxiety on their part, and little or nothing else.

One day one of the wise men of the town, who knew of our predicament, said to my father, "Your son is the intimate friend of the 'schoolboy' Iskander, and I feel certain that if you offered to send your son to the same school which his friend attends, he would go. Try it." My father came home, and, in a half-hearted manner, made the suggestion, and, for the moment, we all laughed. School? For me? My mother, who was somewhat more in sympathy with my aspirations, spoke more seriously of the proposition, and I became interested in it. The moment was of supreme importance. It was one of those moments in which there is much more of God than in the ordinary particles of time. It was the gateway of my destiny, and, most unexpectedly to my parents as to myself, I faced my father and said, "I will go to school."

My decision brought great relief to the whole family, and we all concluded that it was God's will. But when some of our fellow Greek Orthodox heard of it, they urged my father to send me to the clerical school of our bishop and have me fitted for the priesthood, instead of sending me to the heretical Protestant school. That suggestion, of course, proved much more agreeable to my parents. A representative of the bishop resided in the same town, Sûk-el-Gharb, in which the American school was situated, and, since it was necessary for us to go to Sûk-el-Gharb early in the summer and make arrangements for my entering one of the two schools, my father decided that we should interview the representative of the bishop; which we did. My father was very favorably impressed by what he told us about the school. The "holiness of the priestly office" and the spiritual security and certainty of salvation which "the Holy Church of our Fathers" insured to us weighed very greatly with my father, but not so greatly with me. My friend Iskander was a Protestant, and I could not think that he would be damned for it. Besides, he knew a great deal more than our parish priest did. Of course, I had no thought of becoming a Protestant myself, but I craved more learning than the clerical school of our bishop could give.

Upon leaving the representative of the bishop, I decided that I would not go to the clerical school. Its twenty students looked to me "as tame as girls" — Syrian girls. We proceeded to the home of the American missionary, discussed the matter with him, and, finding that I would be accepted as a student if I came in the autumn, I decided to enter the American school.

A STONE-MASON

When it became known in Betater that I was to forsake my father's trade and become a "scholar," the news created a sensation among all classes. It was the "talk of the town" for several days. "Just think of it! Abraham, the Master's son, is going to school, at the advanced age of seventeen!"

CHAPTER VI

A NEW LIGHT

It was in October, 1886, that I was admitted to the American boarding-school, known to us as the High School of Sûk-el-Gharb, a village situated on one of a lofty chain of hills overlooking the Mediterranean Sea, about nine miles east of the city of Beyrout.

In making preparations for this important step, the first thing on the programme was an order to the carpenter for a clothes-chest. This was a proud possession, the first earthly object besides my clothes which I could call my own. The carpenter covered the chest with cheap yellow paint which, whenever, however, and wherever I touched it, came off on my hands and clothes. It must have been a very interesting spectacle to see a "green" boy painted yellow.

As for myself, instead of the bloomer-like *shirwal*, used among the Lebanonians, I put on the more genteel *ghimbaz* (a gown which resembles a kimono), an embroidered vest, a silk sash, white stockings, and red slippers, thus giving myself quite a citified appearance. A muleteer, who cheered my way with quaint songs, carried me, with my bed and clothes-chest, to the coveted institution of learning. Upon my arrival I was assigned three pine boards and two saw-horses as a bedstead. That was the first elevating influence of education that I felt. But by force of habit as well as gravitation I found myself twice on the floor in my first night in that American school.

When the supper-bell rang that evening, the pupils filed into the dining-room, where seats were assigned to the newcomers. All remained standing until the senior teacher came in and said grace. That pious act was startling to me. I had seen my teacher, a layman, offer prayer at the opening of every school-day in my childhood, and I greatly enjoyed the little service; but that a layman should "bless the food" was altogether at variance with my religious antecedents. Only the priest had the authority to lift his consecrated hand and bestow a blessing on such an occasion. Where did the teacher get his authority to perform such a solemn act? With such a question in mind, I could not be reverent during the prayer. I did not bow my head or close my eyes; I looked at the praying teacher with much curiosity as I explained to myself that the entire performance was a peculiarity of Protestantism with which I was not at all concerned. I had come to the school to get knowledge, and nothing else.

It was at that supper that for the first time in my life I occupied an elevated seat at the table. With the exception of a small European-ized minority of them, the Syrians sit on the floor while eating, and serve the food on low tables or large trays. But at the Sûk-el-Gharb school long benches were provided for us to sit on, and as those "modern conveniences" were very hard and had no support for the back, they did not make a compelling appeal to me to forget the more restful custom of my fathers.

THE HIGH SCHOOL OF SÛK-EL-GHARB

A NEW LIGHT

The gospel of "plain living and high thinking," which the Western world is just beginning to discover, was well known to our school. Our supper on that evening, which was a variant of a well-established routine, consisted of boiled potatoes, with the peelings on, ripe black olives, bread and salt. With the Orientals in general, dessert does not rise to the dignity of a course in the plan of the regular meals; it is as irregular in its appearance at the table as a comet is in the firmament. At long and irregular intervals we were favored with a dish of sweets, with the evident intention on the part of the school authorities that we would appreciate the favor. We always did. But while our food was plain it was sufficient to keep us in good health and humor, and only now and then some of us big boys felt compelled to bribe the cook to meet us at the back kitchen window with additional and unauthorized rations.

Next morning lessons began. Owing to the fact that my schooling had been so sadly interrupted when I was put to work at the age of nine, I was assigned to a class of "beginners." They were much younger boys than I, and among them I appeared like a giant among pygmies. I was tall, rough, and awkward, with a vague hunger for knowledge. Under the circumstances, it was a great consolation that my dear friend, Iskander, who had just been elevated to the position of instructor, was to be my teacher.

All studies, up to the senior year, were given in Arabic. English was taught as a language. It interested me at once. I looked upon the English *Primer* as the gateway to untold mysteries, and when I was able to say, "Run, mouse, run. The cat will catch you," I felt that I had entered into the exalted circle of the learned.

But the study which assumed supremacy in my mind above all others during my first year in school was that of the Bible. I shall never forget the thrilling charm of my first Sunday-School lesson. Our topic was the story of Elijah's ascension into heaven in a chariot of fire.

A NEW LIGHT

As a Syrian boy I had not the slightest difficulty in believing in miracles. In the minds of my people the miraculous element stands as the very foundation of religion. Our Bible was full of miracles. Our saints, even our priests, worked miracles. Miracles grew under our eyes. But, to me, the wonder of wonders was the fact that the Bible, the great and holy book of our religion, the Bible of which, as a Greek Orthodox, I had heard so much but which I had seen so seldom in the hands of the laity, was now free and open, *even to me*, not only to read, but to study, and to have explained to me, verse by verse, by "learned men"!

Every school-day, for all the scholars, the first lesson was the Bible. It was the Bible, however, not under the microscope of the "higher critics," but the Bible just as it reads. The pupils read the lesson in turn, each reading one or two verses, and the teacher explained the text, as a profound and uncorrupted supernaturalist must explain it.

The ethical distinctions, also, which beset the

more highly cultivated minds in these days with regard to certain portions of the Bible, were unknown even to our teachers. We read the scriptural stories just as they were. They had grown and been recorded in our country. They were the very precipitate of the moral and intellectual atmosphere of our people put forth in the current idioms of the land of our heritage, and all bound together by a divine purpose. Therefore, "What God hath joined together, let no man put asunder."

The great mystery of the Holy of Holies, as it was interpreted by our teacher, made a profound impression upon me. The Holy of Holies symbolized the unapproachable Divine Presence. "The holy place," where the priests ministered to waiting Israel, represented the world and humanity seeking the light. The "veil of blue, and purple, and scarlet, and fine twined linen," which hung between the Holy of Holies and the holy place, symbolized the barrier which was established between God and mankind when Adam fell, and which could be removed only when the promise of a Saviour was fulfilled. When Jesus was crucified on Calvary, and thus "paid the price of sin," "the veil of the temple was rent in twain, from the top to the bottom," signifying the removal of the barrier of original sin and the opening of the way of salvation to all those who come to the Father through the Son.

To me, that was Christian theology in a nutshell. Other explanations of the Bible were indeed precious, but the lesson of the Holy of Holies, a concentrated world of religious knowledge, was my chief treasure.

When I returned home for the Christmas vacation, I was expected to give a creditable account of myself as a student. All my other acquirements seemed to me too insignificant to be compared with my Biblical knowledge, of which, however, my only significant possessions were the interpretation of the Holy of Holies and the story of the ascension of Elijah. So, when a goodly company of friends and relatives came in to greet me, on the evening of my

arrival, and asked me to "tell what I had
learned," the story of the Holy of Holies leaped
spontaneously forth from my mind. Upon my
auditors it had a telling effect. It was amazing
to them "what schools could do." One of my
cousins was so carried away by my portrayal
of the divine mysteries, that, throwing up his
hands in the air, in Oriental fashion, he exclaimed, "My cousin, by the life of God, go no
deeper into learning. I fear you might lose your
mind!"

The Protestant doctrine of the Bible and the
Church was also very interesting to me, but
somewhat disquieting. It threatened my ancient orthodox faith in the authority of the
Church and the mediatorial offices of the saints.
I was taught that the Bible, and the Bible only,
was of divine authority; that church ordinances
were man-made, therefore faulty. Prayer to
the saints, I was told, was "a worship of the
creature in place of the Creator"; the Church
was the company of all believers, and not simply a body of priests; fasting and other legalistic

practices were vain efforts on the part of man
to save himself by his own endeavor, instead of
seeking salvation by faith in the atoning merits
of Christ. I felt especially predisposed to set
my face against Protestantism when it taught
me to give up adoring the Virgin Mary, the
"Mother of God."

The doctrine of predestination, which the
Protestant world is now in grave danger of
forgetting, greatly puzzled my youthful mind.
Our senior teacher was very fond of expounding
this doctrine, probably because its mystery
afforded much scope for speculation. The
favorite text with which the argument in favor of
predestination was most often clinched was
Romans ix, 15–16, "I will have mercy on whom
I will have mercy, and I will have compassion
on whom I will have compassion. So then it is
not of him that willeth, nor of him that runneth,
but of God that showeth mercy." And oh, how
I pondered these words and how I struggled to
discern the purpose of the Eternal in them. Was
I elected? If so, then why should I strive to win

God's favor, when I already have it? But if not elected, why then make the utterly vain effort to change the eternal decree of the Almighty? Though only a boy, I could not help thinking that if my salvation or damnation had been decreed unalterably before the world was made, my life upon the earth could have no significance whatever. But consolation always came from my suspicion that there must be some hidden, more generous meaning in the text which I had failed to discover. Notwithstanding all these difficulties, however, the inscrutable doctrine of predestination proved of use to us students in that when one of our number did that which in the judgment of the rest he ought not to have done, he was stigmatized "a non-elected soul."

My education was not confined to the Bible and Protestant doctrines. I was instructed in arithmetic, in English, in reading the classical Arabic, in grammar, geography, and writing. My more mature faculties led me soon out of the beginners' class to higher grades, and in the latter part of the year I was allowed to attend the class of "essayists," whose essays were heard and criticized by the senior teacher every Saturday morning.

The most startling experience of my first year in school was my "preaching" at the meeting of the recently organized Christian Endeavor Society, which comprised the entire student body and all the teachers. Toward the end of the year, the invitation to exercise this office came to me as a great honor, but it was a crushing one. At the appointed time one of the teachers led the devotional exercises, and then quietly introduced me as the preacher of the evening. It was the first time in my life that I had ever faced an audience. My "sermon," which occupied four foolscap pages, had taken me so long to write that I thought it would take as long to read. I was disposed, therefore, to read it from the pulpit with rapidity. What the sermon was about I have not the slightest recollection, and the manuscript is lost. What I do remember of that occasion is a curious psychological experience.

As I looked down from the platform I seemed to be peering through a powerful magnifying-glass. The heads of my auditors assumed enormous proportions; their eyes glared at me like those of an angry bull, and really frightened me. Nothing whatever seemed normal. It was my subconscious self that read the little sermon, and I "came to" in my seat in the audience, mopping my face violently. Unconscious of all that was going on around me, I turned to one of the boys and asked, "What happened?" "You preached," was his hasty answer, "for about two minutes."

When I went home for my summer vacation, I was received by my family and friends, not only affectionately but with that regard which is accorded seekers after knowledge among all peoples. The fact that my attainments were as yet very meager counted for naught with my people. I was in the path of wisdom, and that was enough. But such honors brought with them great responsibilities. I was supposed to be able to give an enlightened opinion on

A RICH MAN'S HOUSE

every subject under the sun, from a problem in subtraction to medical questions and the policies of the European nations. Letter-writing for others was probably the most unwelcome distinction my "scholarship" brought me. At that time those of the people of our town who could read and write were numerous, but my friend Iskander and I were the only "school-men" who could *yunshi* (do original work in letter-writing). The calls on me to perform such a duty were not very frequent, because letter-writing has never been nearly so common in the East as in the West. The difficulty of the task lay in the fact that I was supposed to divine the thoughts of the sender of the message, as well as to express them in just the phrases he or she would like. For example, Yusuf's wife would come to me with a few of her relatives and neighbors, and beg me to write a letter for her to her husband. Yusuf had been away from home for a long time; he had sent no money to his wife nor information as to when he was coming home. The family had been living on credit all this time, but could secure credit no longer. The Easter season was fast approaching, and the children were in dire need of a few holiday garments, if for no other purpose than to prevent the suspicion on the part of others that the little ones were destitute. Of these and other matters Yusuf's wife would like to have me write to her husband, but her pride does not allow her to tell me all that in plain terms; I am supposed to be enough of a genius to know her circumstances.

I sit down on the floor, fold my legs, placing the right one over the left, rest my left hand, in which I hold the sheet of paper folded once just below the line where the letter should begin, on my elevated right knee, dip my reed pen in the brass inkstand, and proceed to write, from right to left. Yusuf's wife and her friends sit around me and, with evident admiration, watch my dexterity. I write the "preface" addressing the absent Yusuf as "our father-in-law's son," which is a more modest form of saying "our[1] husband." I convey to him all "becoming respect"; ask the Almighty Father to compass him with his grace, to grant him health and strength and bring him back to his family laden with the fruits of his labors; tell him that, if he condescended to ask about his family, all of them are at this date in happy good health, the children's faces are like the full moon, they lack only the privilege of seeing his face and kissing his hand again; and so forth, and so forth.

"Now, Yusuf's wife, what more shall I write?" I ask.

With her palms open toward the sky and her perplexed eyes moving rather swiftly between my face and the ground, she says, —

"Well, tell him — tell him — well, you know, — God's blessing come into your heart, you know, — as you might say; what is all your learning for?"

---

[1] What must seem rather strange to Americans is the Syrian custom of saying, as a mark of humility, "we," when "I" is meant.

"But," I speak again, "I don't know exactly what you wish to write to your husband, for I am not your confessor."

Here one of the neighbors claims attention and says, —

"Tell him that his wife needs money, and that Abu-Tanûns, her chief creditor, is making her life miserable; he wants his money; tell him that, my soul, tell him just that, and a little more."

Another neighbor, "No! don't write such a thing to him; these people [pointing to the others present] don't know anything; Yusuf knows that his wife needs money and that Easter is approaching, and —"

Another neighbor, "Don't howl so; if he knows all that why does n't he send money to his needy wife? You seem to talk like an ox. Now [turning to me], you, my eyes [an endearing term], write, write and spare not."

The contentions of the many friends of the needy family bring out the exact circumstances, and I proceed to finish the letter without further assistance. The message completed, I throw some dust or sand over the page to "dry the ink," fold the paper, take a tiny bit of bread, wet it in my mouth, seal the missive with it, and hand it to Yusuf's wife, who carries it to the muleteer who is to start the next morning on his journey to the region where her husband is, "before the rising of the morning star."

It was a source of gratification to my parents, and to the pious among our neighbors, that, notwithstanding the fact that I had spent a year in a Protestant school, I had not departed from my Mother Church. During that summer our little parish had the rare privilege of a visit from the great Patriarch of Antioch, who was then on a pastoral tour through his ancient see. Aside from the stupendous prestige of his official position, he was a personal friend of the Sultan, and so, wherever he went, the governors of the provinces were little more than his servants. The entire population of our town and the neighboring villages went out to meet him.

The men of our church formed themselves into
an armed escort, firing salutes all the way and
enveloping the entire procession, Patriarch and
all, in clouds of smoke and dust. I was equipped
for the occasion with a pair of flintlock pistols
and a more modern double-barreled shotgun,
and my place in the procession was close to the
white horse of His Eminence.

At such times as this I felt myself to be as
yet a true Greek Orthodox, but when I returned to the ordinary routine of worship in
our village church, I discovered that the Protestant virus had gone deeper into my blood
than I had been aware of, or desired. My soul
was rent in twain. Sentimentally, I was still
Greek Orthodox; intellectually, I had leaned
perceptibly toward Protestantism. The pictures of the saints on the walls of our church
seemed to me less rich in spiritual mystery than
they did before I went to school. Saint-worship
and many church ceremonials appeared beset
with question-marks. *They had no warrant in
the Bible,* and my inquiring mind chafed under

their claims. Such issues were perpetually in my mind, and I was inclined to argue them with my parents or even with the priest. The priest, however, who was very ignorant and quick-tempered, had very little to say excepting to rebuke me for emulating the methods of "those accursed Protestants who know nothing else but to argue."

With all our differences, however, I managed to retain my respect for the priest until he led me, by his own arrogance, to think and act differently. After my return from school, I no longer observed fast-days and days of abstention from meat. One evening, as ill-luck had it, the priest called at our house and found me eating meat on a forbidden day. He was violent with rage. "What are you eating, you accursed of God?" he said. "You are neither sick nor feeble. Why do you sin in this manner?" Shaking with anger, he advanced toward me and lifted his foot to kick the table from before me.

In an instant I was on my feet, deeply insulted and greatly angered. I told him to leave the house instantly, else I should drive him out with a stick.

My parents were inexpressibly shocked. While they regretted his indiscretion, they were horrified at my conduct toward "the priest of my people."

"My son, my son," exclaimed my mother, after our visitor had gone, "the priest may be a bad man; still he possesses the mystery of the priesthood."

"The mystery of the priesthood!" cried I. "Cursed be he and his mystery! A bad man cannot make a good priest. Mother, I am a Protestant upon the housetop." [1]

My second year at school found me very happy and successful in my studies, but my lessons did not compare in significance with the general, indefinable influence which my school associations exerted over me. I seemed to awaken and absorb revolutionary religious and social forces. My individual life began to

[1] A common Syrian expression for avowedly or completely.

SUMMER COOKING OUT OF DOORS

acquire both retrospect and prospect. I began to feel intelligently the impact of the past and to have visions of the more significant future. My teachers spoke encouragingly to me of my swift progress — "a youth who had but very recently forsaken the barren life of the stone-mason and taken up the duties of the student."

It was during the autumn of this year that I joined the Protestant Church. (Happily we knew no denominational designations in that school, which, however, was of the Presbyterian persuasion.) The American missionary, the Reverend Theodore Pond, who was the principal, examined me and received me into church fellowship. This step I took upon my own responsibility. I knew my parents would not favor it, so I did not ask them. Protestantism seemed to me more reasonable than my old form of faith. It did away with many church ordinances which had often bewildered my growing mind, and it afforded me a closer communion with Christ, who was the only Saviour of the world. Above all things, Protestantism opened and explained the Bible to me, and laid much emphasis on religion as life. When I was being examined by Mr. Pond, he asked me what my parents would think of the step I contemplated taking.

"They would oppose it," I answered.

"Would you disobey your parents?" he asked.

"In this case I would," said I. "The Master has said, 'He that loveth father or mother more than me, is not worthy of me.' Therefore Christ stands above earthly parents."

Mr. Pond was pleasantly surprised at the quick but authoritative answer, and expressed the hope that my parents might, in the not far future, see the wisdom of my course.

My friend Iskander and I were the only Protestants in Betater, and while we were not persecuted in a mediæval sense, we had to fight many battles in defense of our faith. When we came in collision with intelligence, we were no mean fighters, but in the face of benighted bigotry we were often helpless. At such gatherings as weddings and funerals we suffered not a little. We were referred to sneeringly as "the Lutherans, the followers of the lustful monk who ran away from the Church in order to get married." We were urged to admit the truth of the assertions that the Protestants who refused to confess their sins to the priest went up and confessed to the stone-roller on the housetop. Many of our leaders, so they said, held communion with Satan. Our marriage service, being performed by a "lay-preacher,"[1] was invalid. Therefore, Protestant children were bastards, and so forth. Of intelligent criticism we seldom heard a word. Therefore, the reviling of our theological enemies only strengthened our hold on our new belief. Our own families accepted our defection from the faith as one would the inevitable, and parental and filial love kept us generally at peace.

While I was at school, I heard much about

[1] The ordination of a Protestant minister does not, according to the Greek and Catholic churches, invest him with the authority of apostolic succession.

America. I studied its geography, heard of its great liberator, Washington, and almost every Sunday listened to Mr. Pond and other preachers speak of the zeal of its people for missionary work among the heathen of the earth. What has seemed very curious to me, in the light of subsequent knowledge, is the fact that America was always presented to my mind as a sort of hermit nation. Its people were rich and religious and little else. Every one of its citizens told the truth, and nothing but the truth, went to church every single Sunday, and lived the life of non-resistance. America had neither fleets nor armies and looked to England for the protection of American citizens in foreign lands. I do not remember that the missionaries spoke of America in exactly such terms, but by drawing their illustrations always from the religious side of American life, they led many of us to form such views of the New World.

But more exciting tales about America came to me through returning Syrian emigrants. Most of them, being common laborers, knew, of course, very little of the real life of America. They spoke only of its wealth and how accessible it was, and told how they themselves secured more money in America in a very few years than could be earned in Syria in two generations. More enlightened accounts of the great country beyond the seas came into Syria through a small minority of a better class of emigrants. From such descriptions I had a few glimpses of American civilization, of a land of free schools, free churches, and a multitude of other organizations which worked for human betterment. The fact that a few poor Syrian emigrants who had gone to America had in a few years attained not only wealth but learning and high social positions — had become real *khawajas* — appealed very strongly to my imagination. I would go to America if some turn of fortune made that possible.

CHAPTER VII

THE SCHOOL TEACHER AND THE EMIGRANT

At the end of my second year as a student my father told me that he was no longer able to keep me in school. He was getting old fast; his building enterprises grew smaller every year, and of his twelve children six still remained at home to care for. He had already paid twelve Turkish pounds for my two years' keep in school. Adding to that the loss of my wages for two years, his financial burden was no light one. Disappointment fell upon me with the weight of a calamity. I could not blame my father, so I was the more helpless in dealing with the stubborn difficulty. What was to become of me? Was I to be forced back to the circumstances against which I had rebelled so successfully two years before? Were all my hopes to be dashed?

During that summer and autumn my father met with serious business reverses, and we were actually reduced to want. The approach of the winter, always dreaded by the common people of Syria, was doubly dreaded by our family. I had never known what real want was before, and now, after I had been flattered lavishly by my teachers and fellow students as "one of the very promising young men," to behold our family in the grip of real poverty and to think of myself as the helpless victim of such circumstances, was almost unbearable.

Early in November I made a visit to my beloved school in Sûk-el-Gharb and called on Mr. Pond. He asked me interestedly about my plans and listened with sympathy to my story. I told him that my chief desire was to return to the school as a student, but that my father's circumstances rendered this impossible. It was beyond Mr. Pond's power to extend me financial assistance, but he offered me the position of a teacher in the primary or day school, which joined the High School, suggesting that in that position I could avail myself of many of the privileges which the High School offered. I promptly accepted, and in a few days assumed my new duties with great enthusiasm.

The salary of my new position was three quarters of a Turkish pound (about three dollars) per month and my board, which was provided at the High School. My bed stood in my schoolroom, among the benches of my pupils, and served as a comfortable seat for me during recitations. I do not remember that I ever received my salary at the end of the month without a sense of insult. Mr. Pond lived in a beautiful residence. He had a carriage, a saddle horse, and three servants. Why was it that I should accept a position whose salary did not enable me to preserve my self-respect? Yet I had accepted it of my own free will, and I only was to blame for the choice.

My career as a school-teacher covered three years — two in Sûk-el-Gharb and one in the city of Zahlah, which is situated on the eastern slopes of Mount Lebanon, on the main road to Damascus. At that time Zahlah claimed a population of about twenty thousand souls, and enjoyed a commanding commercial position. The city was rich, and its population contained not a few college men, my associations with whom proved very profitable. It was in Zahlah that I first came in touch with the mystery of photography. To me the process was a grand revelation, and I felt greatly exalted when I put on my worsted *shirmal*, Kashmir vest and sash, held a book in my hand, and sat for my picture.

My advent as a teacher in a city school, while I was yet more of a stone-mason than a schoolmaster, must seem to any American "School Board" to have been rather a strange phenomenon. However, it was not so strange as it might seem. In those days and in that country we had no "system" of education, no "teachers' convention," no "parents' committee," and no one thousand-and-one pedagogical devices. Nor did we have a public opinion to back up the nobler idea (if such an idea did exist) that the method of teaching should be such as to develop and maintain mutual sympathy and mutual respect between teacher and pupil. Each teacher was his own Froebel, with Froebel's methods left out. The American missionary would map out a very elastic plan for a school, and leave the teacher master of the situation. Women teachers were as rare as women preachers are in England, and the men found tender patience in teaching school to be extremely slow of results. My own method of teaching was very simple; there were certain lessons to be learned, and the pupils had to learn them. Did I rule by love or by fear? Well, it all depended on the circumstances. The man who wrote, "He that spareth his rod hateth his son," was my countryman, and I was in deep sympathy with him; so also were the parents who had committed their children to my care. And while love was not wholly ignored, I did not very often allow myself even to seem to "hate" my pupils for the sake of undue economy in the use of the rod. It is possible that the punishment of certain pupils might have been excessive and that of others too light, but the *average* was just right, and the response of the children to the stimulus was most gratifying. No lessons I ever assigned to them proved too hard for them to learn. In the mean time the purely social relations between teacher and pupils were always very cordial. Those bright boys even brought me presents; but whether those gifts were marks of appreciation of my services, or bribes, I cannot now tell.

But as a teacher in a Christian missionary school I was supposed also to be ready and willing to exercise the function of a "local preacher," and, on necessity, conduct a simple church service after the apostolic fashion. Only twice during my three years of school-teaching did I avail myself of the privilege of preaching, once in Sûk-el-Gharb, where I spoke again before the Christian Endeavor Society to a better advantage than I had done two years before, and once in the city of Muallekah, a twin sister of Zahlah. This last experience was rather trying. It was on a Sunday evening when I was asked to supply the pulpit of the small Protestant church in that city. With another youth, who was my assistant in the Zahlah school, I proceeded to Muallekah, prepared to conduct the full church service and preach a short sermon. When the time arrived for the service to begin, besides my assistant there was only one worshiper in the sanctuary, a woman. Nevertheless, as one commissioned to proclaim the message of the Gospel on that Sabbath evening, I ascended into the pulpit and began the service, hoping that other worshipers would soon come in. I gave the invocation and read a hymn, which for obvious reasons was not sung. No other worshipers arrived. I read the Scripture lesson and offered the "long prayer." When I opened my eyes I found that the woman, who must have felt very lonely, was asleep. Certainly the time was not very opportune to do great evangelistic work. I dared not look at my assistant for fear he might burst out laughing. But be it said to his eternal credit that that youth continued in a most reverential attitude until I had read another hymn and pronounced the benediction. And I did not blame him a particle for his laughing terribly all the way home, and for telling me that if I continued to preach to such huge congregations, in a very few years Protestantism would sweep Syria.

During my school-teaching period I applied myself to the search after knowledge with strong and sustained zeal. Owing to the scarcity of books, my range of subjects was very narrow. The Arabic language and literature absorbed almost all my time and effort. I mastered its grammar and rhetoric, read extensively in its literature, and committed to memory hundreds of lines of poetry, chiefly from the ancient classical poets. When I became able to write correct poetry, in classical Arabic, I considered the prize of my educational calling won. My absorption in this study led me to neglect the English language entirely. It ceased to have any charms for me, and gradually became a faint and tarnished memory.

In my last year in Sûk-el-Gharb I touched the fringe of Occidental life at two points. First, I acquired a European costume. European dress was slowly becoming the attire of the new "aristocracy of learning." When I first donned this fashionable but strange garb, I was ashamed to appear where people might look at me. The lower half of my person felt quite bare and my legs seemed uncomfortably long. The habit of sitting on the floor often asserted itself unconsciously, and occasionally endangered the seams of the newly acquired costume. My townspeople most uncharitably called me "the man in tights." Happily for me, I only put on the strange garb on special occasions, and retained with it the Turkish fez as a connecting link between the East and the West.

My other touch of Occidental life came from dining with the other teachers one evening at the home of the American missionary. Here it was that I heard the piano for the first and last time in Syria, and ate with the knife and fork. The chief dish of the occasion consisted of a

MR. RIHBANY AT 21

Taken at Zahlah. The first photograph

stratum of dough baked over a dissected chicken. When my plate reached me heavily laden with the strange composition, I was not a little puzzled to know how it was to be eaten. I deemed it wise to follow the example of the others, but to disengage the flesh from the bones of a chicken, with knife and fork, was a painful experience to me. Lacking skill, I applied force, when suddenly my awkward eating tools slipped, and almost broke the plate. I was deeply impressed with the gracious dignity of my host, who appeared not to notice it, while my fellow Syrian guests (I suppose because of our familiarity with one another) snickered at my distressing experience.

My three years of activity and intellectual endeavor as a school-teacher, while they proved advantageous in many ways, failed to put me on the highway of true progress. My salary kept me on the level of poverty, and the opportunities for promotion were extremely scant. I began to realize that soul-expansion and a useful career in the world of knowledge depended first and last, not on the theories of the schoolroom, but on the enlightened and progressive genius of a nation. I could claim no nationality and no flag. The rule of the Turk, especially during the reign of the ruthless Abdul-Hamid, was painfully repressive. Under it love of freedom and of progress was a crime against the State. The hawk-eyed detectives of the tyrant infested the land and haunted with fear the souls of our influential, forward-looking citizens. To those of our people who deemed obedience to authority the greatest virtue, living under such conditions was on the whole agreeable. But to those of us who had tasted the fruits of modern knowledge and been led by it to read greater meanings in human life and to crave a larger and freer intellectual and social environment, the existing order seemed like an iron cage against which our wings beat in vain.

I woke up intellectually only to find that in my own country the European enjoyed far greater political and social privileges than I did;

that nothing was really secure in a land where the ruler maintained a firm hold upon his subjects by promoting divisions and instigating massacres among them. I never saw a manufactured article bearing the stamp of a native factory, nor had I known an inventive genius to be met with anything but suppression. Our schools were simply foreign colonies, tolerated by the Sultan because of the Great Powers which stood behind them. The enlightened youth of the country not only lacked the opportunities which call forth and develop the nobler human qualities, but were constantly watched by the Government as possible revolutionists. With a multitude of other young men I longed and prayed inwardly and silently for better things, or, at least, for the opportunity to emigrate from a country in which life slowly but surely grew to mean intellectual and moral death.

Whither should I go? On one occasion Mr. Pond suggested to me to enter the ministry in my own country. He thought I was qualified by nature for the sacred office, and lacked only the training, which I could have, free, in the theological department of the Syrian Protestant College in Beyrout.

The offer did not appeal to me very strongly. The preachers I had listened to in school, including Mr. Pond himself, made no strong impression on me. Their messages were almost wholly formal statements of doctrine, whose dynamic power decreased in proportion as they were repeated from Sunday to Sunday.

My answer to Mr. Pond's proposition was that I had never contemplated entering the ministry, nor did I feel at the time inclined to entertain such an idea. We both "hoped" that in the future I might be led to take such a step. My hope, however, was a mere imitation of his, for the matter dropped from my mind soon after I left his house.

At last I concluded to continue teaching school, preferring, however, to return to Zahlah, where I had worked during my second year as teacher. Early in September, 1891, I went thither to visit some friends and more particularly to apply for my former position as a teacher.

Upon my arrival I was told that two young men, who had been close friends of mine, were to leave for America the following morning. The news startled me. Certainly I must go and bid them good-bye. Soon after supper I called at the home of one of them and found them both there. We fell on one another's neck and kissed in Oriental fashion.

Speaking both at once, they said, "Abraham, why don't you go with us? What is there in Syria for a man like you? Come, let us go to America together."

The words of my friends, while they stirred violently the depths of my soul and awakened a thousand slumbering hopes, rendered me speechless.

"Why don't you say yes?" they asked. "Let nothing stand in your way, and let us make the voyage together."

"How can I go," I said, "with so many obstacles in the way?"

"What obstacles?" queried my friends. "If your chief difficulty is financial, we stand ready to lend you all the money you need until you reach New York. What better chance can you ask for?"

The moment seemed to me of divine significance. Really, what better chance could I ask or hope for? At last America was within my reach. Would it be anything short of madness to let such a great privilege go by? I had to act on my own responsibility, but I remembered that when I dropped my tools as a stone-mason and went to school, I had to act on my own responsibility; when I left the Church of my fathers and became a Protestant, I had to follow my own course. Now I was called upon to make a third great decision, and to make it quickly. The wiser powers within and above me again asserted themselves, and I decided that I would go to America. Our final plan was that I was to return home at once, secure all the money I could, and, within two days, join my friends at Beyrout, whence we were to sail for the New World.

Betater lies about halfway between Zahlah and Beyrout, and about three miles to the south of the carriage road which connects Beyrout with Damascus. My friends and I were to travel together the next day, until we reached the branch road which led to my home town, where I was to part from them, with the hope of rejoining them at the specified time in the great commercial city on the shore of the Mediterranean. The required change in the programme of my visit to Zahlah was very simple; my friends had already engaged two horses to carry them to Beyrout, and all I needed to do was to hire a similar mount for myself. It was a bit amusing to our whole company when the owner of the horses said that he could not find a "real" horse for me on such short notice, but would give me a *kedish* (a pack-horse), which is not considered an elegant mount by the élite of the country. But the owner said it was

"very light," — that is, a good traveler, — and
I was willing even to be carried on a rail on
such a happy journey.

Shortly after midnight we mounted our thor-
oughbreds and followed the winding carriage
road from the neighborhood of Zahlah up the
eastern slopes of Western Lebanon. On that
highway of Syrian trade and travel the night
was enchantingly alive with caravans, trains of
mules and donkeys, flocks of sheep and goats,
and groups of pedestrians. With the crashing
of hoofs and shuffling of feet mingled the jing-
ling of camel bells, braying of donkeys, bleating
of sheep, and quaint, romantic, many-dialect
human songs, to all of which we added our own
happy, youthful melodies. We reached the
summit of the mountain just as the purple
banners of the advancing day began to stream
over Eastern Lebanon, light the heights and
render the gloom of the valleys more majestic.
From that lofty summit my eyes beheld for the
last time a scene of unsurpassed glory. To the
south arose the giant, hoary head of Mount

Hermon, the aged sentinel of the Promised Land; to the east the storm-splintered peaks of Anti-Lebanon screened the region of Damascus from our sight and extended north to the land of Hamath and the Orontes. The plain of Buk'a lay between the two Lebanons, covered with its rich, grayish-brown, post-harvest mantle. To the west the eye followed the slopes of Western Lebanon to the charmed land of the Phœnicians and the borders of Sidon and Tyre, and rested within the vast curve of the horizon over the blue deep of the Mediterranean. Like the last look at a beloved face that scene remains with me a vivid and entrancing memory. I never can repeat Harriet Beecher Stowe's lines, —

"Alone with thee when purple morning breaketh,
  When the bird waketh and the shadows flee," —

without recalling the compelling vision which filled my soul on that morning on the summit of my native Lebanon.

We dismounted for breakfast at the *Khan* of Dher-el-Beider — an inn of historic fame in that locality. Hanging in the archway of the famous inn were part of the carcass of a sheep and a goatskin full of thick *leben*. Do you know what *leben* is? It is milk soured artificially,—not with chemicals, however, but with a yeast of its own kind. It is thickened by being put in a white muslin sack, or a goatskin, and thus drained of its water. This delicacy, which is being slowly introduced into this country, is so dear to the Syrian heart, and has been for ages, that the Bible counts it as one of the precious assets of the "land of promise" by saying that it flowed, not with "milk," as in the English translation, but with "*leben* and honey."

We did not ask whether the mutton before us had been "inspected"; that was none of our business. We simply ordered broiled meat and *leben* for our breakfast. The innkeeper instantly obeyed; he cut off a chunk of meat, cut it up in small squares, strung the same on slender iron rods, broiled them over a charcoal fire, and served the breakfast, apparently with as much laudable pride as, on similar occasions, thrills the heart of the most elegant housekeeper.

But what I recall now with no little amusement is the way we tried, while our horses paced westward, to sketch the map of our destiny in the New World. The fact that of the country in which we were trying to plan our future we knew very little more than the name did not seem to weigh much with us. The absence of concrete facts upon which to base inferences, and the uncertainties of the future and an unknown country are, as a rule, no real hindrances to the flight of Oriental fancy. Now we would think of ourselves as occupying positions of distinction and honor, blest with riches and culture and far-reaching influence. Then again, suspecting that we might be assuming a little too much, we would clothe ourselves with real humility, and, with unanimous consent, pledge ourselves to "take whatever came in our way," because a haughty heart is never pleasing to God. Now and then a faint flicker of wisdom would intrude upon our earnest deliberations and we would say, in a chorus, "Wait until we get to America."

It was at that point, which has been named since by the authorities of the Beyrout-Damascus Railroad (which at the time of our trip did not exist) "Behamdûn Station," that I dismounted, surrendered my modest horse to my friends, who took it with them to Beyrout, and continued my journey to Betater afoot, with hope and fear struggling violently in my breast.

My return home on the very next day after I had started on a two-weeks visit to Zahlah was a shocking surprise to my mother. "My son," she exclaimed, "*kheir-in-sha-Allah* (may all be well by the will of Allah), what brought you back so soon?" "Nothing but *kheir*, mother," I answered. "I am going to America." A veritable shower of interrogatives — "How?" "When?" "With whom?" "Why?" "With what are you going to America?" — and so forth — fell from my mother's lips. I told her the story in as attractive a manner as possible and begged her to place no obstacles in my way. My father was at once sent for; he quit working and came home to counsel with us. While my sudden decision was a great surprise to my parents, it was not altogether unpleasant. They had confidence in me because I was "a learned man." They regretted deeply my having to depend on others for funds, but it all seemed to them Allah's will. Pushing her scarf back from her forehead and lifting her eyes and hands to heaven, my mother implored the all-seeing, all-wise Father, whose will it was that her favorite son should be torn away from her arms, possibly forever, to guide and prosper him, and return him safe to his father's house.

The problem of a *teskara* (passport), without which I could not legally leave the country, next confronted us. It was no easy matter to secure this legal document, and the time at my disposal was very short. I never can think of the story of my *teskara* without at least taking notice of the belief that "great events cast their shadows before them." During the summer which had just closed I happened to be at Bet-Eddin, the capital of our province, on a visit to a schoolmate whose brother was influential in government circles. During a conversation on the subject of emigration that official asked me whether I had any intention of leaving Syria, if the opportunity offered itself. I answered that I had the intention, but doubted whether such a thing could happen for a long time to come. He stated very graciously that as the *teskara* problem was no small one, he should be glad to arrange matters in such a way as to make it easy for me to secure the necessary paper. "But," I answered, "the law requires that I make my application in person and provide two witnesses to identify me." "Yes," he said, "but I will take care of all that. Let me have your name, destination, description, etc., and when you need the *teskara*, send to me for it." The offer was altogether too attractive for me to reject it and I gladly complied with my influential friend's request. My destination was to be Alexandria.

So when the pressing need for a *teskara did* come, I called one of my father's men and said to him, "Elias, I will pay you double wages to-morrow, if you will go to Bet-Eddin (a six hours' journey on foot each way), deliver this letter to Salim Effendi, and bring back the answer and whatever other papers he will give you. You will say not a word about my going to America to any one else but him." I do not know in what one of the small hours of the night Elias started on his momentous journey. What I do know is that my intense anxiety about the *teskara* made the day seem endless. Whatever I was doing, the *teskara* was in my mind which brooded constantly over the questions: "Suppose Salim Effendi should happen to be absent from home, or that he should fail to secure the longed-for paper without my presence in court in person, or that the court should not be in session?" "If the *teskara* failed to come, should I give up going to America, or expose myself to the penalty of an unjust law and to being disgraced by trying to leave the country as a fugitive?" However, the beneficent powers seem to have been in control, and all my fears were drowned fathoms deep when shortly after supper my faithful messenger appeared at the door dripping with perspiration and covered with dust. Knowing how anxious I was to secure the *teskara* he had it out of his pocket, and, as soon as my eyes met his, threw the precious document into my hands. "Well done, Elias!" I shouted; "may God increase your offspring!" Elias was paid double his wages (sixty cents) and given his supper, including a big glass of wine, besides.

All the money which my father could give me amounted to three napoleons. He wept because he could find no more. It required no very long time to complete my preparations for the voyage. My clothes were tied up into a bundle in a large bandanna. My "bed for the ship" was much like that of the man who was sick of the palsy, consisting of a cushion, a pillow, and a light quilt. With such an equipment I rejoined my friends at Beyrout, at the appointed time.

SCHOOL TEACHER AND EMIGRANT

Our most important task was to secure the indorsement of our *teskaras* — by the Beyrout officials. Difficulties were often placed in the way of emigrants from Turkey by the officials for the purpose of extorting money from them. Emigration to America was discouraged and generally supposed to be prohibited. Our passports indicated that our destination was Alexandria, which was true, but not the whole truth. Moreover, our more refined speech and manners seemed to remove us, in the minds of the officials, from the ordinary class of emigrants. For the indorsing of our passports we were required to pay half a *madjidy* — Turkish dollar — each, and we thought our exit from the unbeloved empire was rather cheap.

Our opinion was probably suspected, for shortly after we left the wharf, our boat was halted and an officer demanded our *teskaras*. The inspector appeared stern and doubtful. Our own boatman advised us to "present" the inspector with half a *madjidy* each, and avoid more unpleasant things. We heeded the advice and the boat went on. When we were within a few yards of our steamer another haughty inspector interrupted our progress and demanded our *teskaras*. Another "half a *madjidy* each" gave us our freedom. We left our "mother country" with nothing but curses for her Government on our lips.

Our steamer tickets entitled us to passage from Beyrout to Marseilles as "deck passengers" — the equivalent of the steerage on Atlantic liners. With more gayety than wisdom we established our quarters high up on the foredeck. There were more sheltered places, but we scorned them.

Joppa was our first stopping-place. Next came Port Said, where a large contingent of Russian Jews joined us. This little city seemed to me a wonder. A department store, a mere toy compared with the department stores of America, dazzled me. Its large glass windows and a real sidewalk around it quickened my poetic sense. I seemed to myself to have come face to face with some of the wonders of the

THE TESKARA WITH WHICH MR. RIHBANY
LEFT SYRIA

world, and my pen spared not in describing the scenes before me.

Alexandria came next, and Port Said was dwarfed in my imagination. I tore up the description of the department store and proceeded to poetize the great city of Alexander.

Shortly after we left this port for Marseilles, the Mediterranean began to be unfriendly. Our quarters on the foredeck, our trunks and bedding, caught the copious spray from every wave. Our gayety changed to grave concern, and all our singing ceased. A peculiar ailment also seized me just below the diaphragm. With our portable beds in our arms we sought more sheltered places, but found them all filled with an inhospitable crowd of Jews and Gentiles. In our extremity, we resorted to a malodorous recess on the port side of the lower deck where many trunks and bundles of clothing had been thrown for shelter, and where ducks and other feathery fellow creatures were kept within wire screens. The ducks gave screams of terror because of our intrusion, and we did no less, because of their presence there. Other human beings joined us in that locality, and we all lay piled on top of that heap of freight, across one another's bodies, much like the neglected wounded in a great battle.

An incident which occurred in that hole (which I have called ever since "the duck apartment") still lives in my memory, because of its amusing and ethical aspects alike.

Lying across my legs, and barely within shelter, was a very kind-hearted, God-fearing man from Damascus. I was just telling him not to allow another person to come in with us, because we were almost suffocated as it was, when we heard a woman approaching us, uttering in the Egyptian dialect terrible imprecations against the steamship company.

I felt that a veritable terror was about to visit us, and very ungallantly called to him, "By the life of Heaven, don't allow this woman in here!" In a second she was upon us, and demanded accommodation.

SCHOOL TEACHER AND EMIGRANT

"*Lewajeh Allah*"[1] (for the face of God), said the kind-hearted Damascene, and squeezed himself a few inches to one side. In an instant the wrathful Egyptian wedged herself in, squirmed round until she secured the proper leverage, and then kicking mightily with both feet, pushed the beneficent Damascene clear out on the wave-washed deck!

When we landed at Marseilles I could hardly credit my senses. Everything Turkish had disappeared and I was walking the streets of France, the great country of which I had heard so much. My friends, having studied at the Syrian Protestant College, besides having a fair knowledge of the English language, knew some French, by the aid of which we escaped on many occasions from the hands of interpreters and ticket-brokers of our own nationality.

In Marseilles I first saw electric lights, which fascinated me beyond description, and there I

[1] By this expression the Orientals mean, for no earthly reward. The good deed is cast Godward, and finds compensation with Him.

first marveled at a railway train. I narrowly escaped being run over near the railway station, when I dashed across the track, a very short distance from an incoming train. A uniformed man, who, I infer, was a guard, shouted at me so fiercely that I thought he was beside himself. I was not fully acquainted with the fact that a train would really run over a hopeful and ambitious young man. It was in Marseilles also that I first experienced a distinctly Occidental sensation, when I cast off the soft Turkish fez and put a stiff, and, incidentally, ill-fitting, hat on my head.

At Marseilles we bought tickets for New York. We were shipped by train (third-class) to Paris, whence, after a halt of a few hours during which we wandered in the neighborhood of the railway station, — "just to see Paris," — we were reshipped to Havre. Here we were herded in a lodging-house, together with many other steerage passengers, for two nights, and were each of us given a table equipment of tinware, consisting of a plate, two spoons differing in size, a cup, and a knife and fork. On the day of sailing we were marched out to the steamer in the style of well-behaved convicts, carrying our labels in our hats.

The steerage of those days on a second- or third-class steamer certainly fell below the worst tenement house. Hundreds of men, women, and children were herded together in a large and filthy cave in the lower regions of the steamer, under conditions which precluded even the commonest decency. The food was distributed to the passengers in buckets and large tin pans, from which they filled their tin plates and cups, and to the swift was the race.

Fortunately for us "college men," and thanks to the linguistic qualifications of my two friends, who won the respect of the captain, or an officer who we thought was the captain, we were given quarters with a few others in a room which contained three tiers of three berths each, and which was more or less successfully partitioned from the main steerage quarters. We had our full share of the noise and stench of the general surroundings, but we enjoyed greatly the decency of our partial seclusion.

Almost all the way I suffered from that peculiar sickness whose acquaintance I first made between Alexandria and Marseilles. Having seen much better days at home, the diet of the steamer tortured my soul. The lower class of Europeans did by no means appeal most exquisitely to my æsthetic sense. My physical weakness made the uncertainty of my future and my financial difficulties oppressive to me. But hope remained alive, the great New World, the enchanter of my soul, was very near at hand, and the God of my fathers was my God and helper.

On the evening of October 6, 1891, our steamer cast anchor in the harbor of New York, too late for us to disembark. From some Italian venders who had boarded the ship we bought the needful things for the evening repast. Here I ate the first real meal since we had left Havre. A certain meat composite, strongly spiced, proved unspeakably toothsome to me. Upon inquiry I learned that it was called "bologna," which term I rooted deeply in my memory as the first trophy of the New World.

Refreshed and sustained by my savory supper, and exhilarated by the thought of my arrival in the great city of New York, I proceeded to the casting of my accounts. The outcome was not all that could be desired. The figures, which "do not lie," showed that my assets were about nine cents (half a franc) and my liabilities forty dollars, which I owed to my friends. Under those somewhat embarrassing circumstances, I was to face the inspector of immigrants at Ellis Island the following morning.

But the significance of the exact knowledge of my straitened circumstances went with me far beyond the usual depression one feels under similar conditions. I was told by well-informed fellow passengers that on the morrow I stood in danger of being deported because the immigration laws of America required an immigrant such as I was, with no family and no position awaiting him in this country, to give satisfactory evidence that he had no less than twenty dollars (the sum must have been a mere guess) on his person; otherwise he could not be admitted into the United States.

That was decidedly unwelcome information. It took away all the pleasure of my bologna supper. To be deported to Turkey! Just think of it! Had my blossoming hopes come so near fruition only to be blasted? I would not ask my friends for more money. They had already told me that they could lend me no more without endangering their own future. But the situation being of such a peculiar nature, my companions came to the rescue by offering to lend me four pounds "on demand," with which to meet the requirements of the law. I found no reason to reject the offer.

On the following morning, armed with my "short loan," I stood before the inspector, who was a Syrian, with only slight tremors in my knees. He asked me my age, the name of the Syrian province whence I came, whether I could read and write, took down my description, and then, with a smile, asked me whether I was married. I came very near giving myself away when, with a smile broader still than his, I answered, "What should I do with a wife, when I can hardly take care of myself?"

With a very encouraging laugh, he said, "Married Syrian immigrants get on much better in this country than the unmarried."

I do not know now in what connection I quoted two lines of poetry to the genial inspector, and, with more playfulness than wisdom, asked him whether he knew of any *beautiful* damsel in the Syrian colony who would consider the advances of a willing young poet. With another hearty smile, he said, "Pass on, you are all right." He did not ask about money! As we passed out of the building, my merry friends said, "Abraham, your wily poetry served you well this time." With a mixed feeling of relief and anxiety, I returned the emergency loan and held fast my half-franc.

We landed at Battery Place, explored the dock for our trunks, which we discovered in a small mountain of baggage, and proceeded to a lodging-house on Washington Street, the chief center of the Syrian colony in New York.

CHAPTER VIII

IT was no easy task for me on the morning of that 7th of October, 1891, to believe my senses when I first experienced that well-nigh overwhelming feeling that I was really in the great city of New York. As our little party proceeded on across Battery Park up toward Washington Street, I felt the need of new faculties to fit my new environment. A host of questions besieged my mind. Was I really in New York? Was I still my old self, or had some subtle, unconscious transformation already taken place in me? Could I utter my political and religious convictions freely, unafraid of either soldier or priest? What were the opportunities of the great New World into which I had just entered? What was awaiting me in America whose life, as I had been told, was so vast, so complex, and so enlightened? Whatever the future had "of wonder or surprise," it seemed that merely being in the United States was enough of a blessing to call forth my profoundest gratitude.

Nor did I have to wait very long for tangible evidence to convince me that America was the land of liberty and opportunity. On that very evening my eyes beheld a scene so strange and so delightful that I could hardly believe it was real. Sitting in the restaurant early in the evening we heard, approaching from the direction of "uptown," band-music and the heavy tread of a marching multitude which filled the street from curb to curb. Some one, looking out of the window, shouted, "It is the laborers! They are on their way to Battery Park to hold a meeting and demand their rights." That was all that was needed for me to dash out with a few others and follow the procession to the near-by park. I had heard in a very fragmentary way of the "united laborers" in Europe and America, but, while in Syria, and as a Turkish subject, it was almost beyond me to conceive of workingmen in collective moral and political action. The procession was dotted

with illuminated banners inscribed with mot-
toes which I could not read, and the gathering
must have been that of some "trade union."
Reaching the park the crowd halted, and a
huge mass of eager men and a few women faced
the impassioned speakers. What those speakers
said was beyond my understanding. I was a
stranger to the country, the English language,
and the political and social activities of free
men. From some fellow Syrians who understood English I learned that those workingmen
were protesting against certain issues which I
cannot now recall. I was intensely interested
in the conduct of the few policemen present.
They walked about leisurely around that human mass, toyed with their clubs, and seemed
utterly indifferent to all that was going on.
The orderly conduct of the meeting and the
rational way of protesting against wrongs, real
or imaginary, was to me poetry set to music.
How I wished I could return to Syria just for
a few hours and tell my oppressed countrymen
what I had seen in America; just to tell them

of the freedom and intelligence of the American laborer, and of his right and ability to convert parks and street-corners into lecturing platforms.

But my revelry in such delicious fancies could not continue very long. The realization of the fact that my assets were only nine cents and my liabilities forty dollars quickly silenced my muse. My two good friends, having fulfilled their promise to lend me enough money to defray my necessary expenses until I reached New York, could do no more for me than recommend me to Abraham,[1] their townsman and the proprietor of the chief restaurant and lodging-house in the Syrian colony. Their recommendation was decidedly flattering, and it was not their fault that the beautiful picture of my character and attainments, which they put

[1] The Syrians invariably address a person by his given name, prefixing the title Khawaja, or suffixing Effendi, on more formal occasions. The constant use of only the given names in the Bible, such as David, Samuel, Paul, John, etc., shows the antiquity of the custom.

before the proprietor, contrasted distressingly with my actual financial circumstances. The forty dollars that I owed those friends being equally divided between them, I gave each of them a note (attested by two witnesses) for twenty dollars, for six months, they promising to extend the time further, if it was found necessary when the notes fell due.

When I handed the notes to my creditors, and we all understood that from henceforth so far as business matters were concerned each one of us was to go his own way and work out his own salvation, a distressing sense of loneliness came over me. Aside from my two companions I was not aware that I had an acquaintance within a thousand miles. I had the name of a young man whose family I had known in Syria, and who was in business in New York, but I would not seek him. My poverty made me feel as if every Syrian in New York would look upon me as a beggar and shun my acquaintance. It was, however, by a fortunate accident that I met this young man on the street the next day after I landed. Perceiving my need, he offered to lend me a "little money." I accepted a loan of five dollars from him, which sum I vowed I would make last until I found work.

But what I was most keenly aware of when I first went into Abraham's restaurant with my "load of cares," was hunger. My protracted sickness and the lack of suitable nourishment on the steamer had reduced me to a state of starvation. My craving at the sight of food was ferocious. For a whole week, no matter how often or how much I ate, I never felt satisfied. To face such a state of things on a capital of half a franc was by no means conducive to peaceful repose. Soon after I had been introduced to the restaurant-keeper my hungry eyes fell on a dish of *maamoul* — a delicious kind of Syrian sweet cakes — which stood on the counter before him. Asking no questions I reached for one of the cakes and proceeded to eat it, with my eyes fixed on the dish. "Fletcherizing" was unknown to me at the time, the cake swiftly disappeared, accentuating rather than appeasing my hunger. When I was about to reach for another, discretion interrupted the proceedings, and I asked, "How much are they?" "Ten cents each," answered the proprietor. I reached for my half franc and said, "This is all I have." "Never mind," said he, "we will let it go at that."

I turned my back on the rest of the cakes.

I spent my first night in New York at Abraham's lodging-house, at an expense of fifteen cents. Besides my sleeping accommodations I enjoyed the privilege of doing my morning ablutions in a dark hall on the ground floor, where a faucet gave forth a generous supply of cold water. A large cake of coarse yellow soap, and a public towel which bore the marks of extensive use, completed the appointments. Compelled by the circumstances to practice "plain living and high thinking," I planned my first breakfast in the New World so skillfully that it cost me only five cents. It was by no means satiating.

Realizing my helplessness while unable to speak the English language, I sought to "master it" on the very first morning after my arrival in New York. I gazed at the multitude of store "signs" with awe. The variety in the phrasing and lettering bewildered my brain. When should I ever be able to read such hieroglyphics? Certainly I must be up and doing. The only English book I could find in the bedroom was a small copy of the Bible, which belonged to one of my friends. I turned to the Book of Psalms and searched for a very short one of the songs of Israel, believing that a short psalm must consist of simple words. By the eternal fitness of things my hand was led to the One Hundred and Thirty-first Psalm: "Lord, my heart is not haughty, nor mine eyes lofty; neither do I exercise myself in great matters, or in things too high for me. Surely I have behaved and quieted myself, as a child that is weaned of his mother: my soul is even as a weaned child." My two companions helped me to understand the more difficult of the sacred words. They made me understand that the word "haughty" was pronounced *hawty* and not *hufty*; they unsealed to my understanding the meanings of the words "exercise" and "behaved," and, in so far as they themselves knew, they taught me how to distribute the emphasis over the measured lines of the Hebrew singer.

But my economic circumstances did not permit of extensive search for knowledge. To remain content with paying fifteen cents a night for my lodging savored of recklessness; therefore I went about seeking cheaper quarters in the colony. Some public-spirited countrymen, agreeing with me that a stricter exercise of economy was absolutely necessary to my welfare, informed me that another Syrian, whose name was Moses, kept a sort of lodging-house, "good enough for a man in my circumstances," and charged only five cents a night. Certainly that was the place for me, and I immediately sought the proprietor. Moses met me with a cordiality which made me feel as though he and I had been fast friends for years. He explained to me that the chief reason why he provided lodging accommodations over his store at such low rates was to aid struggling Syrian immigrants, such as I was, to get on their feet. He explained also that he managed to maintain his establishment at these incredibly low prices by dispensing with bedsteads, soap, towels, and other luxuries, and reducing the lodging-house business to the absolute essentials. And, since I had a bed (my steamer bed), he thought I would be very comfortable at his house.

I felt somewhat disquieted because of the absence of soap and towels at the new lodging-house, but the saving of ten cents a night was very compelling. It seemed to me, also, that Moses' cordiality ought to be properly valued. Lodging with him appeared to me like "personally conducted" travel. Therefore I hastened back to the more expensive hostelry, took up my bed (tied up in a bundle), and left Abraham and went to Moses.

IN NEW YORK WITH NINE CENTS

The jovial proprietor of the five-cent lodging-house led me up a squeaky stairway in the interior of his store, to a spacious corner off the first landing in which stood a bare board platform, which he most cordially offered to me as my sleeping quarters. The fact that the location afforded me no privacy whatever seemed to Moses to be an advantage rather than the reverse, as it provided me with an abundance of fresh air. I need not fear the intrusion of strangers, Moses remarked, because all those who went up and down the stairs were our own countrymen. Nor need I be disturbed by the noise which the peddlers, who came in to buy goods until late in the night, made in the store below, because I must be fully acquainted with the noisy bargaining of the Syrians. Lastly, in order to make my lot more acceptable to me, the genial Moses added, as he turned to go downstairs, "If you should desire to wash in the morning, be sure to let me know."

Sustained by the sense of honest economy, I spread my bed on the platform and, after casting a comprehensive look at the dingy paper on the walls and at an indescribable back yard, which I could see reasonably well through a small dirt-streaked window, I went out, promising to return after supper.

On my return in the early evening I found that two other boys had secured lodging accommodations on Moses' platform. It was wide enough for three persons, such as we were, under peaceful circumstances. But my fellow lodgers fell into a serious dispute early in the evening, over a charge and a counter charge of stealing, which led them to intermittent fighting until late in the night. As a fellow countryman, and desiring to win the blessing promised to the peacemakers and, incidentally, a little much-needed repose, I made some attempts to restore peace between them. The nature of the belligerents, however, was such as to convince me that the vigorous urging of my arbitration measures would very likely cause them to unite their forces and attack me.

As I lay awake under Moses' roof that night

IN NEW YORK WITH NINE CENTS

I thought of all the good things I had ever
enjoyed in my life, of all the poetry I had
learned, of the pride with which my breast had
heaved as a "learned man" among my kindred.
Now I was in the New World, which did not
seem to take immediate notice of my worth,
tucked in a dingy corner, nay, crucified between
two thieves!

I awoke early the next morning with a raging
headache and a stiff neck, picked up my bed,
and returned to Abraham. Moses was very
kind and reasonable when I paid him my night's
lodging and told him that I felt compelled
to seek more comfortable quarters. He even
pledged himself to be very diligent in looking
out for some suitable employment for me in a
Syrian store; and Moses was a man of his word.
But for justice' sake I must not leave Moses'
establishment without telling the whole truth
about it. The reader must not allow himself to
imagine that the only lodging accommodations
that tender-hearted man had was the platform
mentioned above. No; Moses had two real

rooms whose floors were covered with untacked and rather inexpensive carpets, and which he reserved as temporary shelters for immigrant families, a room for a family. I mention this fact not only to do justice to the five-cent lodging-house, but to tell the reader what type of immigrants are found sometimes in such places. On one occasion I called at this lodging-house to see a family of five — the mother, three daughters, and two sons, with one of whom I was very well acquainted. It was a family which had seen better days in the Old World. Both the sons were college men; the mother and the daughters were also partially educated. The father had been a successful business man until certain calamities came upon him and swept away all that he had. His death shortly followed, and left his family destitute. At last the fatherless household managed in some way to reach the New World, with nothing but hope with which to make a new start in life. I felt not only sad but actually guilty when I intruded upon the privacy of such misfortune.

IN NEW YORK WITH NINE CENTS

The downcast face of the mother, as she sat on that crumpled carpet in Moses' lodging-house, and the sad, appealing glances of her eyes, which seemed to say, "You should have known us in our better days," still haunt my conscience. Nevertheless such observations, together with my own trying experiences in those days, have taught me to contemplate the dwellers of tenement houses with a greater measure of respect than I could otherwise do. Not a few of the noble possibilities of future America lie hidden in those dark, musty, shabby dwellings, awaiting the call of this country's wondrous opportunities to resurrect them to the newness and glory of a free and useful life.

The Syrian colony in New York consisted in those days of a few store- and restaurant-keepers, a multitude of peddlers of "jewelry and notions," and a few silk merchants who, although they peddled their wares, bore the more dignified designation of "silk-sellers." For lack of better pursuits, college men often took up silk-selling as a means of livelihood, which occupation, however, required capital and often letters of introduction to the well-to-do American families. My inquiries for something to do precipitated usually the following questions from the older colonists, who seemed to me to be steeped in wisdom: —

"Do you have money so that you can at least buy an interest in a store, or deal in silk?"

"No, I have no money at all."

"Do you have letters of recommendation from missionaries in Syria to persons in this country?"

"No."

"Can you speak the English language?"

"Not so that I can be understood."

"How old are you?"

"Twenty-two."

"Twenty-two! Too old to master the English language. The only thing you could do, and which thousands of Syrians are doing, would be to peddle 'jewelry and notions.'"

Call it pride, vanity, or whatever you please, whenever I thought of peddling "jewelry and notions," death lost its terror for me. The mere sight of those crude, greasy peddlers nauseated me. Come what might, I would not carry the *keshah* (a colloquial Arabic name for the peddler's pack).

The period of painful suspense, which seemed to me to cover a whole year, lasted in reality only twelve days, at the end of which I found employment. During those twelve days, when not searching for work, I spent my time exploring New York, which overshadowed my soul like a vast mystery. I made my first appearance on Broadway on a Monday morning. I shall never forget the almost overwhelming impression which that great thoroughfare made upon my mind. The amazingly wide sidewalks were solid streams of humanity. Compared with the leisurely, swaying gait of Orientals, every one in that vast multitude seemed to be running. How limpid and how quiet that human mass appeared! No disputes and no demonstrative bargainings at the doors of those great stores! No shouting, "Ho! your back!

your side!" as in Beyrout. Almost complete silence prevailed, and the stupendous concourse of men and women moved as swiftly and gracefully as a perfectly adjusted and well-oiled machine.

I soon realized that while I was *in*, I was not *of*, New York. I was afraid to do anything, even to walk freely, for fear of jarring the harmony of the surroundings. The memories of the Turkish soldiery which haunted my soul made me fear every uniformed man I saw. I felt instinctively constrained to stand at attention whenever I passed a policeman. Men wearing silk hats inspired me with reverence. The close resemblance of this type of hat to the headgear of the Greek priests made me conclude that the wearers of the towering headdress were all preachers, and confirmed in my mind what I had heard in Syria about the profound and universal religiousness of the American people.

Like a newly born babe, I needed to be completely adjusted to the new environment. In fact, it was neither to my interest, nor to that of New York, for me to act freely in public before I was properly trained. I remember very clearly when I went out to post my first letter in the great metropolis. I was directed by wise counselors to deposit the letter in a red iron box fastened to a post on the sidewalk. Reaching the first box of that description, I took hold of a shining handle and gave it a sharp turn. It was the fire alarm. An alert policeman, motioning to me vigorously with his club to stop turning the shining handle, ran to me, and, leading me to a letter-box, pointed out with some earnestness the difference between the fire-alarm box and the receptacle for missives.

Another strange situation confronted me when I visited the office of a New York business man, on the third day after my arrival in the city. One of my companions on the voyage had a letter of introduction to this man from a friend in Egypt, and we deemed it necessary that the three of us should visit the New Yorker and present the message to him in a body. Upon coming into the office building a boy admitted us into a little room — all made of iron — and closed the door. Seeing no open door anywhere in that room I suspected some foul play. What! have I come to the great New World to have a mere boy play such a trick on me? As I was about to seize the little culprit and demand the release of the whole party, the entire room, floor and all, began to ascend. Then I remembered that in Sûk-el-Gharb, Syria, a few years before, one of the missionaries, while delivering an illustrated lecture before our school, had shown us the picture of a New York building, and told us that the Americans have such means of vertical transportation.

Additional impressions of New York which puzzled my unacclimated brain in those days I find in the fragments of a correspondence I had with a friend in Syria, and which was in part as follows: —

"New York is three cities on top of one

another. The one city is in the air — in the elevated railway trains, which roar overhead like thunder, and in the amazingly lofty buildings, the windows of whose upper stories look to one on the ground only a little bigger than human eyes. I cannot think of those living so far away from the ground as being human beings; they seem to me more like the *jinnee*. The second city is on the ground where huge armies of men and women live and move and work. The third is underground, where I find stores, dwellings, machine shops, and railroad trains. The inside of the earth here is alive with human beings; I hope they will go upward when they die. There are so many big policemen who don't seem to be doing anything. The women walk on the streets freely, dressed like queens. They wear very thin veils, for the purpose, I believe, of showing rather than hiding their beauty, for they look magical. But they don't speak to anybody. The other day, while in the great garden called Central Park with a Syrian friend, we needed to know where the animals were (the Zoölogical Garden), and, seeing a lady sitting on a bench, we thought we would ask her to direct us. After our more sociable Oriental custom I ventured to greet her, with a 'Good-morning.' She neither answered nor even looked at me. I was struck with dumbness. But my wiser companion asked her where the animals were without saying 'Good-morning,' and she immediately pointed us in the right direction. They have strange ways here. And you never saw such drinking of intoxicants as there is in this city. We Oriental wine-drinkers do not know what real *effrenj* [1] drunkenness is. I have seen even drunken women raving in the streets, but I am told they are not real Americans, not of those who wear the magical veils. I am trying to know more of this strange, great world and will write more about it."

During my days of enforced and painful idleness in New York, Battery Park was my chief resort. I would spend hours on those

[1] The Orientals call all Western peoples *effrenj*.

benches, either writing poetry, generally of a dolorous kind, or studying the many and varied ships which plied the deep before me, or picturing to myself the greater distress which I thought awaited me when my five dollars was all spent. But Battery Park stands in my memory associated with much holier thoughts than these, for it was there that a spiritual vision came to me unique in my experience. It is, I believe, chiefly because of that vision that throughout my ministry I have preached with unshaken faith and unreserved devotion the precept that "man's extremity is God's opportunity."

Feeling deeply depressed and disheartened, late one afternoon, I strolled down to the famous park. The sea and sky were very beautiful, but I seemed to have no share in their beauty; I appeared to myself to be a fugitive in an unfriendly world. I sat on a bench and cast a vacant look on the world before me. I felt very lonely, and longed, as a babe, for my mother. But as the sun began to fade away from the sky, I began, as by a miracle, to feel an inward supply of power and courage. The beauty of the sea and sky seemed to have been made for me; I was owner of all that I saw. I seemed to myself for the moment to look upon the world through the mystic eyes of my Oriental ancestors, and see it, so far as a youth could, as the garment of God. Surely the Father was with me. "Why art thou cast down, O my soul, and why art thou disquieted in me? Hope thou in God." I remember with perfect clearness that I said audibly, "The God who created me and these wonders before me will never forsake me," and arose and walked like a strong man.

Now you have the privilege of explaining this experience as "an uprush of reserve energy from the subconscious realm," or as "nervous reaction," or whatever else you please. What *I* know is that the abiding worth of an experience ranks higher in the world of real life than that of any philosophy *about* it. From that day to this, notwithstanding the fact that I have often stumbled and fallen, doubt in God's providence has never secured a hold upon my mind, nor do I remember that I have ever failed to trust that He is mine and I am His. In my extremity in a lonely world, without Bible, preacher, priest, or sacrament, I came into living, first-hand contact with the Eternal Reality.

CHAPTER IX

My very recent friend, Moses, did not forget his promise to be on the lookout for a position for me in some Syrian store, for on my tenth day in New York he sought and found me in Battery Park, and, with a generous smile, told me of a merchant who needed a *katib*, — bookkeeper, — and Moses thought I was the man for the place. Realizing that I had never had any experience in bookkeeping, he instructed me not to be overconscientious in confessing my ignorance, for he was certain that I could do all the bookkeeping that the merchant needed. The customers of the store were peddlers of "jewelry and notions," who did business on very simple lines, and almost all the transactions were carried on in the Arabic language. If at long intervals some orders came to us in *El-Angleezy* (English) Moses promised to come and help me fill them in the proper manner.

BOOKKEEPER AND EDITOR

In company with my beneficent friend I proceeded to No. 5 Carlisle Street, the store of Khawaja Maron, where the position of *katib* awaited me. Moses introduced me to the proprietor as "one of the most efficient bookkeepers he ever knew," and departed. Maron told me that the salary of the position I was seeking was twenty dollars per month, and that I would be expected to perform the usual duties of a *katib*. I accepted the offer with gladness of heart, promising to be at my "desk" at seven o'clock the following morning.

Recalling the time when as a school-teacher in Syria my salary was three dollars a month and my board, twenty dollars seemed to me a species of "frenzied financiering." I had always known the position of *katib* to be most conducive to dignity and elegance, and an excellent opportunity for advancement in the commercial world; therefore I had every reason to imagine that my new position at 5 Carlisle Street was the gateway to riches and honor.

Before seven the next morning I was at the

store. The proprietor, who slept in a room in the rear end of the building, was just out of bed and about half-dressed. He greeted me very pleasantly, although his appearance just then, and the fact that he slept at the store, cooled my ardor considerably. After lighting a cigarette, he handed me twelve cents, explaining that my first duties in the morning were "to go down to the corner," buy a scuttleful of coal for ten cents, a bundle of kindling-wood for two cents, carry the ashes out and deposit them carefully in the barrel on the sidewalk, build a fire in the stove, sweep the store and the sidewalk, see that the boxes of goods on the shelves were in proper order, and then take up my clerical duties. It was not so much the *quantity* as the *quality* of the programme that pierced my heart with many sorrows. Was this what it meant to be a *katib*? Was this what I had come to America for? Whatever it was, necessity was laid upon me to humble my pride and accept the situation. Did I not consent to the spirit of the One Hundred and Thirty-first

Psalm, my first scriptural lesson in America, when I repeated reverently, "Lord, my heart is not haughty, nor mine eyes lofty"? The seemingly menial tasks of my new office came, perhaps, to test the sincerity of my prayer.

I applied myself to my duties as *katib* most conscientiously. My broom searched the remotest and darkest corners of the store, and, as it seemed to me, made the sidewalk in front of it the envy of our neighbors. The boxes of "jewelry and notions" stood on our shelves in as straight lines as any courses of stone I ever laid as a stone-mason. Even Khawaja Maron noticed the orderliness and cleanliness of the surroundings and pronounced them "exceptionally good," and I was really proud to have it known by every one who came into our store that it was I who put the establishment in such order.

Our store, however, was put to other uses not strictly commercial, which the social habits of our Syrian customers demanded. On rainy days it fell to me to entertain groups of peddlers who sat around the stove, smoked cigarettes of "Navy Tobacco," and indulged themselves in their simple but boisterous pleasures. At times they would buy a wash-pitcherful of beer and drink to one another's health out of one common glass. They would offer the "learned *katib*" a foaming glass of the beverage, which was invariably refused.

But at those informal social gatherings around Maron's stove more significant events occurred. At times my guests, the peddlers, would ascend to the consideration of rather weighty subjects. From the prosaic counting of the combs, pipes, razors, necklaces, and other commodities which each of them had sold on a certain day, they would rise to the poetizing of the prowess of their Syrian feudal lords and the miracles of their saints. "Khawaja Ibrahim," Dhieb would ask me, "which is the greatest nation in the world?"

"I have always thought," I would answer, "that England was the greatest nation, but they say here that America is the greatest."

"Of course you will say that," said Tannûs, "because you are 'Brustant' [Protestant]. France is the greatest nation. The French protected us from being massacred in 1860, and what have your England and America done? May Allah save the fiery French! They terrorized the hearts of the Mohammedans and the Druses when the army of Napoleon came into Syria." Here Maron, just to please me, would speak with some gravity from behind the counter, "You, Tannûs, must not be so rude as to contradict the *katib;* he is a learned man, while you are but an untaught commoner." That was always enough to vanquish my opponent, and keep the integrity of my "learning" unimpaired.

Certainly American customs did not escape serious consideration by my friends the peddlers. Almost all of them being illiterate, and having no access whatever to real American life, their discussions of it, as I now recall them, were most interesting exhibitions of human psychology. The universal rule that the untrained mind makes the most sweeping deductions from the slightest contact with facts received around Maron's stove most emphatic confirmation. Some of those simple-minded peddlers of "jewelry and notions" had succeeded in observing that domestic and social life in America was not so homogeneous as in Syria, that in this country the individual was much freer and much more sharply defined. Consequently nothing remained to prevent the conclusion that the Americans lived a life of completely detached individualism. Members of the same household lived a life of mutual exclusiveness. "Hear, and I will tell you," said Abdu, especially to new arrivals from Syria; "in this country the husband and wife live each one alone. He has his room and she has hers, and, if anything, the man has to mind. They say that he has to knock at her door like a stranger, and she does n't have to let him inside if it does n't suit her. He has to say 'Shkooz me,' which means, 'Forgive me'!"

"But how can they live that way and raise

children?" Anton would inquire. "*Ya Allah* [O God], what customs! Give me Syria and its submissive women. Where are you? — let me tell you, our country knows something. Woman must be kept in obedience or she would lead man to all sorts of trouble as Eve led Adam in Eden. I say, give me Syria, the mother of mankind!" Then some genius in the crowd would do human nature no little credit by remarking, with a vigorous waving of the hand, "Get out of here! Your words are empty. No matter how they live, the Americans look clean and well-fed, and we are dirty and hungry; shorten your speech until you know what you are talking about."

On one occasion Maron offered the store to one of his customers for the celebration of a genuine Syrian wedding. The offer was accepted and our commercial establishment resounded with joy. Other than Syrian dwellers of the neighborhood flocked to doors and windows and feasted their souls on things which their eyes had never before seen nor their ears heard.

We seated the bridegroom (the bride was in another building) in the place of honor — behind the counter. Beer and *arak* flowed like water. The men sang *aataba* and the women *zelaghet*, and we all partook of a bounteous feast which was spread on benches, cases, and chairs, while the straight rows of boxes of "Fine Combs," "Collar Buttons," "Baby Rattles," and so forth, looked down upon us from the shelves with Occidental serenity.

My salary of twenty dollars a month did not prove so ample for my every need as I had at first thought it would. Only by the strictest economizing was I able to secure food and shelter and other necessities at an outlay of only fifty cents a day, which left me but five dollars a month as a sinking-fund with which to pay my debts and fortify myself against accidents and sickness. I had only two suits of clothing, one of which I reserved for Sundays. The winter was fast approaching and I had no adequate clothing for it. I envied every man I saw wearing an overcoat. Being already forty-five dollars in debt, I resolved that I would borrow no more under any conditions. Compared with the temperature of Syria, the cold in New York was as much of a revelation to me as the skyscrapers. How to keep warm out of doors was a question which I could not safely evade. By the advice of a well-disposed acquaintance I bought a coarse, heavy shirt which, I was told, was made of camel's hair, and therefore very warm. I was glad to renew my acquaintance with the camel, even though in such a roundabout way, as well as to bear some resemblance to John the Baptist; but the coarseness of the shirt militated strongly against all my ideas of refinement. It was, however, my chief means of defense against the rigor of my first winter in America, my memories of whose blasts remain keen and clear.

Notwithstanding my humble position as *katib*, I was not long in New York before I began to dream dreams and see visions. How to acquire the priceless privilege of being an American citizen, was the first and foremost question in my mind. I was told that I did not need to be in such a hurry about this matter, but I thought differently, and on November 18, 1891, not quite six weeks after I landed at Ellis Island, I appeared in the Court of Common Pleas of the County of New York, accompanied by an interpreter, and asked to be "admitted into American citizenship." My heart never thrilled with holier emotion than when I assented to the oath of allegiance, "that it is *bona fide* my intention to become a citizen of the United States and to renounce forever all allegiance and fidelity to any foreign Prince, Potentate, State or Sovereignty, and particularly to the Sultan of Turkey of whom I am a subject." I felt such an inward sense of relief and exaltation that my countryman, the interpreter, appeared to me to be an alien. It seemed to me at the moment, although of course not so clearly as it does now, that by that act I had forever broken the shackles which had bound me and my forefathers for ages to the chariots of tyrants, and had become a citizen of a coun-

CITY HALL, NEW YORK

Where first naturalization papers were taken out

try whose chief function was to make free, enlightened, useful men.

I soon also made the acquaintance of the few college men in the Syrian colony, foremost among whom stood Khawaja Najib Arbeely, the Syrian inspector of immigrants at Ellis Island, who examined me upon my arrival in New York. Being eager to enjoy the privileges which in the Turkish Empire we never dared even to talk about, I proposed the organizing of a society whose purpose should be the mutual benefit of its own members and the advancement of the various interests of the Syrians in general. The suggestion met with favor among the leaders of thought in the colony, and the "Syrian Scientific and Ethical Society" was organized. Mr. Arbeely was elected president and, to my amazement and notwithstanding my shirt of camel's hair, I was elected vice-president. It is never an easy task to bind a large number of Syrians together in any enterprise. The oppression under which they have lived for ages has well-nigh crushed all public spirit and initiative out of them. The lifters being the very few, any attempt among them at collective action of any sort is beset with grave difficulties. But our proudly titled society flourished for a time beyond our most extravagant expectations. My deep interest in it, and in what I thought was to be its future, made me eager to serve it in almost any capacity. The subjects of our debates and discussions were large and various. History, philosophy, the good and evil of immigration, the greatness of the United States of America, the superiority of the Syrian to the Irish population of Washington Street, — these and many other subjects called forth the impassioned eloquence of the orators among us, who spoke with perfect confidence and freedom, and often regardless of the facts.

It was very interesting and gratifying to me to observe that at the meetings of the society discussions of American life occupied a much higher level of thought than at Maron's store. The response of the enlightened minority among the New York Syrians to the challenge of American civilization, while by no means revolutionary, was encouraging. Now and then gleams of a new light shot through the speeches of those who had touched with intelligent sympathy the borders of America's higher life, and exerted on me an awakening influence. On one occasion a speaker undertook to portray the superior aspects of American civilization. He began in an eloquent manner to describe the extent and the material achievements of the country as they were known to him. He called our attention, first to the "wonders of New York," such as the Brooklyn Bridge, the skyscrapers, the department stores, the newspapers, etc. Then he gave a vivid picture of the vast railroad, telegraph, and postal systems. From that he proceeded to speak in poetic terms of the schools and the churches and kindred interests, until he came to his climax whose thrilling effect I still remember with grateful appreciation. "Sirs," said the orator, "do we fully appreciate the fact, we who have come from the land of oppression and petty aristocracies, that in this country the humblest man is called 'mister,' and the highest title is that of 'gentleman'?"

I was expected to make an "oration" at any time and on any subject. Being one of the very few in the society who could speak the classical Arabic in extemporaneous address, I was looked upon by many of my fellow members as a "real orator," and credited with such a wealth of knowledge as would have dwarfed the resources of a Herbert Spencer. My most impassioned appeals in those "orations" were for the stronger cohesion of the Syrian population in the great city in which we lived, and the endeavor on the part of our people to adopt the noble principles of American civilization, of which, however, I knew nothing at the time.

The headquarters of our society were established at Abraham's restaurant. He and his partner Abu-Khalil permitted us to hold our meetings at their eating-place on condition that, after every regular session, on Wednesday evening, those of the members who were really interested in the welfare of the society should purchase at least one plate each of a spread of Syrian sweets, such as wheat starch cooked with grape molasses, rice cooked in milk and sugar, and other dainties, which Abu-Khalil served with incredible promptness after it had been "moved and seconded to adjourn." Abu-Khalil's anxiety to "do business" during the sessions greatly interfered at times with the proceedings. His customers came in at all hours, until late in the evening, and they had, of course, to be served. While our orators were toiling to round out their telling periods, Abu-Khalil would sit behind the counter smoking his *narghile*. Utterly unmindful of the significance, at least to the speaker, of an approaching climax, he would interrupt at the most critical moment by shouting orders into the kitchen. I particularly recall one meeting of the society at which Abu-Khalil's interruption was perfectly shocking. The subject of the principal speaker was "The Glory of Ancient Syria," and his purpose was to prove that that country, which is now oppressed and unproductive, had given the world many of its most precious possessions. "Our Phœnician ancestors," declared the speaker, "invented the alphabet, manufactured glass, carried on a vast commerce with Egypt, and planted colonies on the western shores of the Mediterranean. Our Arabian ancestors invented algebra, developed the science of medicine and chemistry, and excelled the world in poetry. On the looms of our Sidon and Tyre were woven the purples of the Roman Cæsars, and it was in our country that the crowning glory of all human possessions " — Abu-Khalil into the kitchen, "One dish of stuffed squash for Khawaja Abdu-Allah, and one grape molasses for Khawaja Toufeek." — The speaker, "the Bible, the Word of God, was revealed!" That seemed to the rank and file of our members, not only an annoying interruption, but downright sacrilege. Abu-Khalil, however, was not an impious man, and no one could justly suspect that he did not say his prayers daily before going to bed. His disturbing conduct during some of our meetings was simply the result of mental specialization in business during waking hours. When we, the officers of the society, came to remonstrate with him upon the matter, he gave us a very simple, direct, and manly answer. He said, "You *ulama* [learned men] are after science and philosophy, but my business is to sell *matbukhat* [cooked goods]." God and Mammon could not be served together. "The Syrian Scientific and Ethical Society" was driven out of Abraham's restaurant, and, after some wandering and vain searching for a suitable shelter, perished.

While the untimely death of our society was a severe disappointment to me as one deeply interested in the welfare of the Syrian colony, individually I had every reason to be grateful for the results of my activities in it during its brief existence. I won the confidence and respect of my countrymen, which seemed to raise the level of my life and make me forget for the time being that I was a poor youth

clothed in garments of camel's hair. After
hearing my first "oration" at one of the meetings, my employer, Maron, was so favorably
impressed that on the next morning he informed
me that he had added five dollars to my salary,
declaring with childlike sincerity that he had
never imagined that his *katib* was so "learned."
His breast heaved with pride when many of our
countrymen besought me to write letters for
them to their feudal lords in Syria, "in my
profound classical Arabic." A month later he
added another five dollars to my salary, promising, also, to give me a share in the business
if I would agree to stay with him permanently.
Friend Maron further concluded that I was too
good to sweep the store, which duty he assigned
to a peddler who lodged in the back room in the
building.

All that was, indeed, glory and honor, and
some money for me. But after having spent
three months with Maron I discovered unmis-
takably that I was not made for a commercial
career. I never could remember the prices of

things from one day to another, while it was no effort at all for me to commit to memory a score of lines of poetry by reading them only two or three times. To listen to those peddlers talk with gushing enthusiasm and satisfaction about how much money they had made on their trips, was really painful to me. Being in business for the sole purpose of making money appealed to me very faintly, even in my poverty. The ideal side of life gripped mightily at the strings of my heart. There was no idealism in the selling of hair-brushes, pipes, cuff-buttons, and the like, therefore I did not deem it the proper occupation for me.

While in such a frame of mind I was most naturally eager to accept another position which was offered to me early in the spring, and which seemed to me to combine both the commercial and the ideal aspects of life. About that time Mr. Arbeely, the president of our Scientific and Ethical Society, began the publication of "Kowkab America" (the "Star of America"), the first Arabic newspaper ever published in the

Western hemisphere, and offered me the position of literary editor. He stated that my utterances in classical Arabic at the meetings of the society, and the public spirit which permeated them, convinced him that I was the man for such a position, and he hoped I might accept it.

With difficulty I restrained myself from shouting for joy. Was it possible that I was to occupy the commanding position of an editor, to become the fashioner of public opinion, so soon after my arrival in America? Certainly the supreme opportunity of my life had come; the open road to the realization of my hopes and ideals was now before me. My salary was to be the same at the start as that which I had been getting as *katib*, with the promise of a substantial increase in the not very far future. I was to be provided with comfortable lodging accommodations in the office building on Pearl Street, and to have exclusive quarters, all my own, as the editor, from whom much was expected. Desirable as a larger income was, it appeared to me to be only a minor matter. The dreaming idealist in me had the upper hand of the prudent and practical commercialist.

The office of editor offered imperishable rewards. It meant intellectual expansion, moral and social victories, leadership of public opinion, and, in this case, perhaps the inauguration of a political movement in free America, which might at least mitigate the tyranny of the "unspeakable Turk" in our mother country. Last, but not least, was it not very probable that by virtue of my position as editor I would in due time be admitted to the circle of editors of the great New York dailies, and thus come in close touch with the highest and best in the life of America?

"Dreams are true while they last, and do we not live in dreams?" Woe to that youth who does not dream on a large scale. My expectations were not only laudable but commendable. I accepted Mr. Arbeely's offer the very day after it was made, promising to take up my duties in about two weeks.

My exalted opinion of the office of editor and its social requirements made me shed my camel's-hair shirt and buy a real white stiff-bosomed American shirt, a turn-down collar, and a four-in-hand necktie, ready tied. That was as far as I could go in acquiring suitable wearing apparel for my new office, and it really seemed to me a big step forward in my social evolution. During my career as *katib* I had shared a bed with another man in a Syrian lodging-house, at an expense of fifteen cents a night for both of us. Our room was possessed of a peculiar type of odor, which neither my bedfellow nor I knew how to modify. When I accepted the new position it did not seem to me that that room was the most suitable lodging for the editor of the first Arabic newspaper ever published in the Western hemisphere, even for the two weeks, at the end of which I was to enjoy the comforts of a more desirable environment. I dissolved partnership with my bedfellow immediately and in a businesslike manner, leaving to him all the bedding I had brought with me from Syria, which had increased rather than decreased by use.

Our newspaper office force consisted of Najib Arbeely, the proprietor, a Damascene; Hbib Patrekian, the publisher, an Armenian; Yusuf Hajj, the compositor, a Beyroutine; and myself. Our journalistic enterprise began most auspiciously. Its advent was celebrated at headquarters by a large company of Syrians and a few Americans, largely reporters. The rooms, which the artful proprietor decorated with rich Oriental draperies, were packed with happy guests, and eloquence flowed no less copiously than beer and *arak*. The New York papers gave generous accounts of our undertaking, and the warm congratulations of educators, poets, and prelates poured upon us from all over Syria.

I was decidedly proud when, upon my arrival at the office to assume my editorial duties, I read on the door of a small room, "The Editor's Room. No Admittance." That was a justifiable and stimulating exclusiveness, which seemed to me to mark the beginning of a splendid career. Soon after my arrival at the office, the publisher presented me with a pack of gilded visiting-cards bearing the proud designation of my office, in both the Arabic and the English, as follows —

ابرهيم متري رحباني

محرر في جريدة كوكب اميركا

A. M. Rihbany,

Arabic Editor
of
"Kowkab America."

My further acquaintance with the headquarters, however, tended to weaken my confidence that I was connected with a great enterprise.

Our offices occupied a small apartment, apparently intended originally for light housekeeping. It consisted of three rooms and a "kitchenette." The proprietor and the publisher slept in the main office, in folding beds which were disguised in the daytime to appear as something else. The compositor slept among his

type-cases, Mr. Arbeely's brother in the kitchenette, and I in my "editor's room." Before many
weeks the compositor rebelled against sleeping
in the "type-room," where the smell of ben-
zine, oil, and paper threatened his health. By
the direction of the proprietor he moved his
bed into my room "temporarily." Soon after,
the brother of the "boss" discovered that it was
utterly impossible for him to secure sufficient
rest in the kitchenette, which was the wash-
room for all the office force, and wondered
whether he could not be accommodated "for
the present" in the editor's room. It was decided by his brother that he could. The three
cots which beset my desk behind and before,
with their complements of clothing and shoes,
were hardly conducive to lofty flights of literary genius. But that was not all. The proprietor's other brother, who was a physician, would
often bring his "special patients" into my room
for examination, and request me to "kindly go
into the other room for a few minutes."

It soon developed also that my duties as

editor had been intended by the proprietor to be as multifarious as were my duties as *katib*. I was required to keep the accounts, to look after the list of subscribers, attend to a large part of the business correspondence, solicit advertisements, do the work of a reporter, and even help fold the papers and prepare them for the mail, besides editing every item which went into the paper.

In these rather distressing circumstances a philosophical turn of mind came to my rescue. I tried to read the gospel of my destiny in the light of the years, and not the days and months, and to look upon the present difficulties as merely transient. Our enterprise was in its infancy, and as a healthy infant its potentialities were great. The path of success and glory most often traverses swamps and deserts, and those who have the vision of ultimate triumph must learn to endure hardships as true soldiers. I thought of what the proprietor had often told me of the poverty and hard struggles of some great American editors at the beginning of their careers, and often quoted to myself the great saying of Mohammed, "Heaven is under the shadow of swords!" Furthermore, by being obliged to translate the general news from the American newspapers, under the supervision of the proprietor and by the constant aid of the dictionary, I was acquiring a very serviceable English vocabulary.

With such means of consolation in mind I addressed myself to my task, for a whole year, with unreserved devotion and with the determination of a man who was bound to succeed. No Horace Greeley ever wrote editorials with a clearer sense of his own infallibility than I did in the "Kowkab." My objective was no less than to be the disinterested reformer of my people, to whom I directed a series of editorials, brimful of fatherly advice.

I counted it a great honor also when I was sent to interview Dr. Charles Briggs, professor at Union Theological Seminary, when he was being tried for heresy by the New York Presbytery. By the aid of an interpreter I ventured to ask Dr. Briggs whether he still believed in Christ. The Professor smiled quizzically and answered me with a quotation from the First Epistle of John: "'And the blood of Jesus Christ his Son cleanseth us from all sin.'" The interview was "satisfactory," but I still entertain the suspicion that Dr. Briggs, inwardly, treated my pretentious visit to him as a joke.

In the autumn of 1892, when Mr. Cleveland was elected President for the second time, I first made the acquaintance of American politics. The fact that that acquaintance was very slight did not prevent me, as an editor and a youth, from making broad claims to knowledge of statecraft. But how I first became a Republican remains to me a blank mystery. In so far as I can remember I simply woke up to the unaccountable fact that I was an adherent of the "Grand Old Party." And I do not believe that I am the only Republican who is at a loss to know the incentive which first led him to wear the insignia of his party. Suffice it to say, that I am a Republican still, but with ample discre-

KOWKAB AMERICA

The first Arabic newspaper in the Western Hemisphere

tionary power. On the night of the election mentioned above I joined an immense crowd of New Yorkers who assembled in front of the buildings of the great daily papers "to watch the returns." Here again I was happily amazed at the orderliness of the stupendous gathering of people, which seemed to me a glorious vindication of liberty. The comical expressions, the good-natured jeers and shouts of triumph, and the dignified acceptance of defeat were to me a feast of reason.

Hanging from the uppermost story of the home of one of the newspapers were two ladders of equal length, the rounds of each of which represented the exact number of States then in the Union. Immediately beneath the one ladder stood an image of Mr. Harrison, and beneath the other an image of Mr. Cleveland. For every State vote won by either candidate his image was removed one round higher. With great apprehension I watched the upward progress of the Cleveland image, and when it approached the top of the ladder I concluded that the country was doomed. What the issues of the campaign were I had no clear idea; I had only learned from Republican sources that great national calamities were sure to follow a Democratic victory, and I believed the prophecy. When the returns of the election showed a Cleveland victory, I thought to myself that the American people must have committed some grievous sin for which that victory was the punishment.

But on the next day after the election an American young man, who happened to come into my office, undertook to explain to me that the cause of Harrison's defeat was not so mysterious as I had thought. However, my visitor's ideas were expressed in such profound and faultless English that I could understand but very little of what he said. At short intervals he would say, "Yes, sir, Harrison was beaten because he is in the hands of the monopolists, who grab the people's money and put it in their own pockets." The frequent reiteration of this sentence enabled me to apprehend in a general way what it meant, but I had not the slightest knowledge either of the form or substance of the word "monopolists." However, I knew at the time that there was a city in America called Minneapolis, and, therefore, concluded that the *Minneapolists* were the highway robbers my visitor was talking about. I have long ago made a sincere and, I believe, sufficient inward apology to the citizens of the great city of the Northwest.

Unintelligent and superficial though it was, my interest in the political campaign of 1892 had an enlarging effect upon me. It was my first great incentive to ask questions about and to idealize the possibilities of American citizenship. Again I was moved with stronger conviction than ever to renew my appeals in the "Kowkab" to my fellow Syrians to drink the nobler spirit and adopt the customs of free America.

Contrary, however, to my most confident expectations, the proprietor looked upon my policy with disfavor. He contended that my

bugle-calls to the Syrians to follow the path of
American civilization was bound to arouse the
suspicion of the Turkish authorities. The "Kowkab," he said, was meant to be loyal to the Sultan, if for no other reason, because the majority
of its subscribers were residents of Turkey. If
Abdul Hamid should for any reason stop the
circulation of the paper in his empire our whole
enterprise must cease to be. The publisher also
protested against any show of antagonism to
Turkey in our columns, chiefly because his
brother held office in one of the Turkish provinces, and he had written to our office that the
least manifestation of disloyalty on our part
might cost him not only his office, but his liberty as a citizen. That was a severe disappointment to me. The hand of the Turk was still
heavy upon me, even on Pearl Street, New
York.

Apparently the course of my destiny lay in
another direction than that of journalism. The
"Kowkab" did not make the forward strides
I had expected it would. My task as editor

grew harder at the end of the year and less dignified, rather than the reverse. Serious differences occurred between the proprietor and the publisher, which led them one evening to a fist fight. Discord ruled our office, and I concluded to seek new pastures outside New York. By exercising strict economy I had succeeded in paying my debts and buying an overcoat (at a fire-sale) and a new suit of clothes. Otherwise I was penniless.

CHAPTER X

OUT FROM MY KINDRED

IT should be borne in mind, however, that my decision to depart from New York altogether was only in a small part the result of my dissatisfaction with my lot as editor. The real cause lay much deeper. The Syrian colony in New York seemed to me to be simply Syria on a smaller scale. During my stay of nearly eighteen months in it I did not have occasion to speak ten sentences in English. We ate the same dishes, spoke the same language, told the same stories, indulged in the same pleasures, and were torn by the same feuds, as those that had filled our lives on the Eastern shores of the Mediterranean. I seemed to be almost as far from the real life of America as if I had been living in Beyrout or Tripoli. The only glimpses I had of the higher life of this country came to me through the very few enlightened Syrians who mingled extensively with the better class of

Americans, and who only occasionally visited our colony.

The sum total of my year-and-a-half's experience in New York convinced me that it was most difficult, if not impossible, for a foreigner to become really Americanized while living in a colony of his own kinsmen. Just as the birth of a new species can never take place without a radical break with the parent stock, so the thorough transformation of a foreigner into an American can never be accomplished without the complete departure, inwardly and outwardly, of that individual from his kindred.

The Syrian colony in New York rendered me all the service it could by providing me with a home for about eighteen months among those whose language was my language and whose habits were my habits. Its Oriental atmosphere with its slight Occidental tinge protected me from the dangers of an abrupt transition. Had I been thrust into American society upon my arrival in this country, penniless and without serviceable knowledge of the English language, the change in environment might have proved too violent for me to endure with any comfort. To me the colony was a habitat so much like the one I had left behind me in Syria that its home atmosphere enabled me to maintain a firm hold on life in the face of the many difficulties which confronted me in those days, and just different enough to awaken my curiosity to know more about the surrounding American influences.

The "gregarious habits" of foreigners in this country are deplored by those who have the welfare of both the foreigner and America at heart. It is evident to such well-wishers that the congregating of aliens together, especially in the large cities, tends to encourage in them the naturally strong desire to cling to their inherited modes of thought and life, and to make the task of Americanizing them doubly difficult. This inference is substantially correct. Nevertheless the fact remains that, but for these "gregarious habits," a multitude of the less aggressive foreigners, by being scattered prematurely among an alien population, would very likely lose their bearings, suffer disheartening loneliness and dejection, and become public charges. The law of the "survival of the fittest" rules in those "foreign colonies" in American cities, just as it does everywhere else. The multitude of "commoners" furnish the conditions necessary to produce the small minority of eager, aggressive idealists, whose restless spirits soon break through the barriers of inherited customs and respond with avidity to the challenges of a higher civilization. To such the word America soon takes the form of Opportunity, and is understood in terms of incentive and room for soul expansion. The loose composition of a population of many and mutually exclusive nationalities, the grotesque manners, and the multitude of saloons and other haunts of vice and crime in the "lower regions" of American cities, where the foreign colonies are generally located, soon tend to awaken in the mind of that foreigner, who finds himself yearning for a better

order of things, the significant question, Where
is America?

I often asked myself, in those days, where
and how do the real Americans live? Who are
the people who foster and maintain that American civilization of which I hear so much, but
which I have not yet known? I have seen a
multitude of Irish, Italians, Poles, Russians,
Chinese, and other human elements which make
up the community in which I am living, but
where are the Americans? It seemed to me that
in a cosmopolitan city like New York it was
well-nigh impossible for a poor foreigner like me
to come into helpful contact with its real American families. Therefore I would leave the great
city and seek the smaller centers of population,
where men came in friendly touch with one
another, daily. It had been made clear to me
that a purely commercial career could not satisfy me, that I had a deep longing for something
more in the life of America than the mere loaves
and fishes, therefore *that* something would I seek.

But, as has been already stated, at the end

of my year-and-a-half's labors in New York, I found myself almost penniless. I had not enough money to carry me two hundred miles from that city. Whatever my *theory* of the "loaves and fishes" may have been, the *fact* was that I sorely needed them.

It so happened that the most intimate friend I had in America at the time was a young man, a graduate of the Syrian Protestant College in Beyrout, who was engaged by the Presbyterian churches of Pittsburg as a missionary among the Syrians in that city. Amin sent me a most urgent invitation and money enough to come to him. He thought his salary would keep us both, until we had matured our plans for the future. We were "to live and die together!"

Fortune smiled also from another direction. Several Syrian silk-merchants in New York, learning that I was about to leave the colony and that I was in straitened financial circumstances, offered to give me all the silk goods I might want to sell in my travels, "to keep me alive until I found a more congenial occupation," — for which goods I was to pay at my convenience. The selling of silk, or anything else, was really hateful to me, but urgent necessity compelled me to carry with me a small quantity of the fabrics. The Syrian missionary in New York introduced me to the noted Presbyterian divine, Dr. David Gregg, of Brooklyn, who gave me a letter of recommendation. In compliance with wise advice I went also to Dr. Henry van Dyke, then pastor of the Brick Presbyterian Church, and requested his indorsement of Dr. Gregg's letter. Dr. van Dyke met me very cordially, but felt some hesitancy about giving a recommendation to one who was an entire stranger to him. But I said to him, in my broken English, not to be afraid because "*I was very good man*," at which I saw him turn his face from me and smile. Reaching to the bookcase behind him he took out a book of a very strange character and asked me whether I could read that. I said "No. This must be Babylon writing." Shaking with laughter, he said, "It is shorthand." He wrote on my letter,

"I join in Dr. Gregg's wish for Mr. Rihbany's success," and so forth, and dismissed me with a "God bless you."

Armed with those weighty documents, on the strength of which a man of stronger commercial instincts than I possessed might have done much business, I started out of New York. Upon my arrival at the Pennsylvania Railroad station to take my first railway trip in America, the luxurious coaches seemed forbidden to me. Recalling to mind the rough and dingy "third-class" car in which I was shipped from Marseilles to Havre, I thought certainly the plush-seated, mahogany-finished coaches which stood before me were not for penniless foreigners such as I was. Failing to find the humble conveyance I was looking for, I asked a uniformed man, "Which the train to Pittsburg?" Pointing to the train which I had inspected three times, he said, "This." Still afraid of getting into the wrong car, I gazed at the man, who, perceiving my perplexed condition, took me by the arm to the door of one of

those costly coaches and said, "Get in here."
I immediately obeyed, and the moving palace
carried me to Pittsburg, where my friend Amin
and I were to seek as our fortune the best things
in the life of America.

In Pittsburg, where I sojourned for about
two months, Amin and I, like our countrymen
of the primitive church in Jerusalem, "had all
things common." We abrogated the law of private property between us altogether. Whether
of books, clothing, money, or even letters, there
was no "This is mine" and "This is thine";
all that we possessed was *ours*. Oriental senti-
mentalism and brotherly feelings reached their
height with us when we vowed that "so long as
we both shall live, we will have a common
purse and share to the utmost each other's joys
and sorrows." In our sharing the one bed and
eating our meals at a restaurant on one "twenty-
one-meal ticket" there was nothing particularly
interesting to the public. But when we wore
one another's clothes, being different in size, we
attracted some attention.

[250]

OUT FROM MY KINDRED

Our plan for the future was that we would enter college together at the earliest possible date. Amin, as I have already said, was a graduate of the Syrian Protestant College of Beyrout, Syria, but he was wise enough to suppose that there were "more things in heaven and earth" than he had yet learned, and that a course of study in the higher branches of knowledge in one of the leading universities of this country would not, in his case, be superfluous. To secure funds for this worthy purpose we decided to travel in these States, and, wherever possible, lecture before churches and societies on the Holy Land, sell goods, seek financial aid by whatever other honorable means, and, as soon as our financial circumstances warranted, apply for admission at that great university which happened at the time to be nearest to us. My friend, who had a very fair knowledge of the English language, was to be the senior member of the firm. He was to address the large assemblies on Sundays and other occasions, and I, who had never spoken English

in public, was to screw my courage to the stick-
ing-point and address small groups, in parlors
and at prayer-meetings. Our choice of a vocation
was to be made while in college, with the assistance of our professors.

But our fine plan was ere long destined to
fail, and our fraternal vow to be broken. We
started out on our "lecturing" tour in the summer, when the activities of the churches are at
their lowest ebb. We encountered the absorbing excitement of the World's Fair, which was
in progress at Chicago, and plunged into the
memorable financial panic of 1893. The public
mind was not in tune for lectures on the Holy
Land, or any other land, and there was very
little money available in the hands of the public
to invest in Oriental silks. And what I felt was
the severest trial to me was that my beloved
friend, Amin, proved decidedly "infirm of purpose." The least difficulty discouraged him.
He was a complete failure as a public speaker,
and whenever he could dispose of a piece of
silk, he sold it at cost and spent the money in

defraying his expenses. Late that summer, utterly crushed by the many difficulties which beset our way, he left me, for aye, and joined some members of his family who were at the World's Fair.

I was left alone battling against a sea of trouble. However, I made a resolution which never was broken, namely, that, while I longed passionately for that unaffected, juvenile warmth of Syrian friendship, I would enter into no new partnership of any sort with any one of my countrymen. I thought I could hear the same voice which said to my namesake, Abraham, "Get thee out of thy country, and from thy kindred, and from thy father's house, into the land that I will show thee." I renewed my resolution to do my utmost to secure a college education, or in some other way relate myself to the higher life of America.

Shortly after the departure of my friend Amin, my career as a "silk-seller," which had by no means been an ideal success, came to an end. I certainly lacked to a very large extent the sagacity of the merchant. I did not believe in letting the customer "look out for herself"; I deemed it my duty to guard her interests with scrupulous care. I would point out to the prospective purchaser all the flaws in a piece of silk, in advance, believing that the excellencies were too obvious to be detailed. Whenever I was asked whether the goods were all handmade, I would answer that while I was morally certain that they were, "I could not swear to it," because I had never seen the process with my own eyes. Such conduct was not due to the fact that my honesty never was accustomed to failing, but to my theory that the business I was in was mean enough without lying about it. Consequently, the high prices of the goods, coupled with my uncalled-for conscientiousness, were by no means conducive to winning the confidence of would-be purchasers and to doing a "rushing business." I returned the goods to the merchant who had been my source of supply in silks during my business career, and decided to pursue my life's ideal as a "lecturer."

CHAPTER XI

MY struggles with the English language (which have not yet ceased) were at times very hard. It is not at all difficult for me to realize the agonizing inward struggles of a person who has lost the power of speech. When I was first compelled to set aside my mother-tongue and use English exclusively as my medium of expression, the sphere of my life seemed to shrink to a very small disk. My pretentious purpose of suddenly becoming a lecturer on Oriental customs, in a language in which practically I had never conversed, might have seemed to any one who knew me like an act of faith in the miraculous gift of tongues. My youthful desire was not only to inform but to *move* my hearers. Consequently, my groping before an audience for suitable diction within the narrow limits of my uncertain vocabulary was often pitiable.

The exceptions in English grammar seemed

to be more than the rules. The difference between the conventional and the actual sounds
of such words as "victuals" and "colonel"
seemed to me to be perfectly scandalous. The
letter *c* is certainly a superfluity in the English
language; it is never anything else but either
k or *s*. In my native language, the Arabic, the
accent is always put as near the end of the word
as possible; in the English, as near the beginning as possible. Therefore, in using my adopted
tongue, I was tossed between the two extremes
and very often "split the difference" by taking
a middle course. The sounds of the letters, *v*,
p, and the hard *g*, are not represented in the
Arabic. They are symbolized in transliteration
by the equivalents of *f*, *b*, and *k*. On numerous occasions, therefore, and especially when I
waxed eloquent, my tongue would mix these
sounds hopelessly, to the amused surprise of
my hearers. I would say "coal" when I meant
"goal," "pig man" for "big man," "buy" for
"pie," "ferry" for "very," and *vice versa*. For
some time I had, of course, to think in Arabic

and try to translate my thoughts *literally* into English, which practice caused me many troubles, especially in the use of the connectives. On one occasion, when an American gentleman told me that he was a Presbyterian, and I, rejoicing to claim fellowship with him, sought to say what should have been, "We are brethren in Christ," I said. "We are brothers, by Jesus." My Presbyterian friend put his finger on his lip in pious fashion, and, with elevated brows and a most sympathetic smile, said, "That is swearing!"

But in my early struggles with English, I derived much negative consolation from the mistakes Americans made in pronouncing my name. None of them could pronounce it correctly — Rih-ba'-ny — without my assistance. I have been called Rib'-beny, Richbany, Ribary, Laborny, Rabonie, and many other names. An enterprising Sunday School superintendent in the Presbyterian Church at Mansfield, Ohio, introduced me to his school by saying, "Now we have the pleasure of listening to Mr. Rehoboam!" The prefixing of "Mr." to the name of the scion of King Solomon seemed to me to annihilate time and space, and showed me plainly how the past might be brought forward and made to serve the present.

But my struggles with the technicalities of language were not the only pains of my second birth into the new environment. The social readjustments were even more difficult to effect. Coming into the house in Syria, a guest removes his shoes from his feet at the door, but keeps his fez or turban on. It was no easy matter, therefore, for me, on going into an American home, to realize instantly which extremity to uncover.

The poetic Oriental mind extends hospitality in a very warm and dramatic manner. The would-be guest, although able and willing to accept an invitation to dinner, expects to be urged repeatedly by the would-be host, to have all his feigned objections overruled, to be even pulled bodily into the house before he gives his consent. By following such tactics in this country, I lost many a precious privilege. The brevity of the American invitation distressed me greatly. Whenever I was told, "We should be much pleased to have you come in and have dinner with us, if you can," I would answer, "No, thank you; I cannot possibly come," when I had it in mind all the time that I would gladly accept if they would only urge me. But they would let me go! They would take me at my word (as they should not do, I thought, in such matters), to my great disappointment. It was not very long, however, before I became on this point thoroughly Americanized. However, eating butter on bread, dessert with every meal, and sitting in rocking-chairs seemed to me to be riotous luxuries. It took me about three years to become accustomed to these seeming superfluities. It would require six now to make me give them up.

The prominence of woman in domestic and social affairs seemed to me, when I first came in close touch with American society, a strange and unnatural phenomenon. While in Syria, contrary to the view which generally prevails

in this country, the woman is not *considered* a
slave by the man, yet in all important domestic
and social matters she is looked upon as only
his *silent* partner. The American woman is by
no means silent; she finds it neither convenient
nor necessary to assume such an attitude.

The first opportunity I had of making close
observation of the social position of the American woman was at the home of a Methodist
minister where I proved sensible and fortunate
enough to accept "without controversy" an
invitation to dinner. His wife presided at the
table with so much grace and dignity that my
astonishment at the supreme authority she
exercised on the occasion was deeply tinged with
respect. How harmonious the husband and wife
seemed! What mutual regard! What delicacy
of behavior toward each other! But I could not
avoid asking, subjectively, "Is all this really
genuine? Does this man treat his wife in this
manner always, or only when they have company? Why, my host seems to be in the hands
of his wife like the clay in the hands of the pot-

ter! Why should a woman be given so much latitude?" and so forth.

When, later in the evening, upon retiring, the lady said to her husband, "Good-night, dear," and *kissed him in my presence*, the act seemed to me distressingly unseemly. It is no longer distressing to me.

It should not be counted against an Oriental that he is unable in a very short period of time to invest such phases of conduct with high idealism. If his instincts are normal, intimate associations with the better class of Americans cannot fail to change his sentiments and clarify his vision. Not many years will be required to reveal to him the elevating beauty of a woman's being the queen of her home, with her husband as a knight-errant by her side; to teach him that America, as the heir to the noblest traditions of northwestern Europe, has discovered that which neither the Oriental peoples, ancient Egypt, Greece, nor Rome succeeded in discovering, namely, that true civilization can arise only from a mutual regard of the equal rights, and, within the family circle, the mutual love of man, woman, and child.

All such discipline, however, was not to be compared with the economic difficulties which beset my way, put my optimism to the severest test, and seriously threatened my stoutest resolutions. In my travels westward, the expressions, "These are very hard times," "The summer is a dull season for the churches," "Not many people care for lectures this time of year," tortured my hearing everywhere. It was so difficult for me to secure money enough to keep soul and body together. In Oil City, Pennsylvania, I longed for the first time for the "flesh-pots of Egypt" and wished that I had never left Syria. In my search for a cheap lodging-place, I was directed by a police officer to an old house which seemed to me the symbol of desolation. An elderly lady, who appeared very economical in smiling, "showed me into my room" and disappeared. As my weary arm dropped the valise inside the door, every sustaining power in me seemed to give way. Sobs and tears poured forth simultaneously with, "Why did I ever leave Syria?" "Why did I not stay in New York?" "Is this what America has for me?" and other questions with which I besieged the deaf ears of a lonely world. The fact that my hostess served no meals afforded me an excellent excuse to ask her to direct me to a "real" boarding-house. She did so, and I transferred my headquarters to a more cheery dwelling, where the landlady smiled graciously and generously, and the presence of fellow guests helped to lighten my burdens.

The veiling of the future from mortal eyes is, I believe, a divine provision whose purpose seems to be to tap the springs of heroism in human nature and to equip the soul with the wings of hope. Nevertheless, this blessed mystery has its drawbacks. Prolonged uncertainty of the future in those days of loneliness and poverty threatened to sink the goal of life below the horizon and make of me a wanderer in a strange land. The alternation of life between the two extremes, feast and famine, is never conducive to connected planning and constancy of endeavor.

At Columbus, Ohio, I spent a whole week in strenuous but utterly fruitless endeavor to secure opportunities to earn some money. Having had to pay in advance for my week's keep at a very frugal boarding-house, I had only ten cents left, which I put in the "collection plate," at a Salvation Army meeting. To be penniless was not entirely new to me, but as the week drew to a close, the question where I was going to secure money enough with which to leave Columbus became terribly oppressive. There was one more venture for me to make. I had the name of a Methodist minister, the Rev. John C. Jackson, pastor of the Third Avenue Methodist Episcopal Church, whom I had not yet seen during my sojourn in the capital of Ohio. My courageous plan was to call on this clergyman and request him either to give me the chance to lecture in his church for a small financial compensation or to lend me money enough to enable me to leave Columbus. The distance from my boarding-house to his residence measured, if I may trust my memory, twenty-four blocks, which I walked in what seemed to me the hottest day in the calendar of the years.

My general appearance when I arrived at the parsonage was not exactly what I should call a clear title to confidence and the securing of credit. Nevertheless, I made my application with a creditable show of firmness, placing in the hands of the clergyman, who was just recovering from a long illness, my letters of recommendation. He disposed of my request to lecture in his church by saying, "There is no possible chance for the present." When I applied for a loan of five dollars, his pale face lighted up with a short-lived smile as he asked, "Do you expect you will get it?" "Y-e-s," I answered, "and to return it, also." "When would you return it?" he asked again. Falling back upon the Biblical language of my kinsmen, I said, "If God prolong my life and prosper me, I will pay you." Assuming the attitude of perplexed charity, Mr. Jackson said,

"I do not know whether you are the man to whom these letters pertain, nor, if you *are* the man, how you secured them in the first place; but I am going to try you. Here is five dollars." "Certainly God has not left this world," I said inwardly, as I received the money from the good man's hand. It was only a week thence when God did prosper me just enough so that I was able to return to Mr. Jackson his money and I received a letter from him (which I still treasure) thanking me for my "promptness" and wishing me all kinds of success.

The next point I touched at after leaving Columbus was Mount Vernon, Ohio, where I was much cheered, chiefly by the kindness of the Presbyterian minister and his gracious wife. And it was at Mount Vernon that I learned my first memory lesson in patriotism. Soon after my arrival in that town I strayed into the public square where stands a fine soldiers' monument. It seems to me that my attention had never been strongly challenged by a similar object in this country before I reached that

SOLDIERS' MONUMENT, MOUNT VERNON, OHIO

small Ohio city. Certainly I must have seen soldiers' monuments in other towns, but was not ready to respond to their appeal. Here, as soon as my eyes beheld the significant memorial, I forgot for the moment my weariness and poverty and yielded myself to the mighty challenge of the thought that I was in a country where men died willingly and intelligently for their flag and all it symbolized, and that what the flag did symbolize were ideals worth dying for. I was chained to the spot until I had committed to memory the inscription chiseled on one side of the granite base, and which read —

OUR COUNTRY

By that dread name we wave the sword on high,
And swear for her to live — for her to die.

These vital words have clung to my memory, in the exact form quoted above, for over twenty years. When I thought of including them in this story, fearing that my recollection of them might be incorrect, I wrote to the commander of the Grand Army post of Mount

Vernon, requesting him to send me an exact copy of the inscription, and upon comparing it with my memory picture I found that I was only slightly incorrect in that I had in the first line the word "In" in place of "By," and the word "lift" in place of "wave."

Perhaps the choicest of the events of my Wilderness-of-Sinai discipline since I had left New York, occurred at Elyria, Ohio. I reached that town late in the evening with a very small sum of money in my purse — something less than two dollars. The severe economic struggles of the immediate past had taught me to be abnormally cautious in spending money. Failing to secure accommodation at either of two cheap boarding-houses in the town, I ventured into a hotel with very noticeable timidity. As soon, however, as the clerk told me that my lodging there would cost me seventy-five cents, I departed. I had the name of a prominent minister in the town on whom I thought I would call first, and, if he promised me the opportunity to lecture in his church, I might feel free to indulge in the luxury of lodging at a hotel.

My experience with that divine was not pleasant enough to permit of the mention of his name and denomination. When I stated my case to him, he assumed a decidedly combative attitude. I was so weary that I should have been most grateful for a few minutes' rest in one of the many upholstered chairs which graced the living-room, but the elderly gentleman stood in the door and kept me standing in the hall, while he quizzed me as follows:—

"Did you say that your purpose in lecturing in the churches is to secure funds to go to college?"

"Yes."

"Well, I doubt it. I have seen many fellows such as you. What college do you expect to enter?"

"I do not yet know, but it will be some good college."

"You don't even know what college you expect to enter? I can say one thing for all of you 'traveling students.' You are very cunning."

"But I can show good letters of recommendation from ——."

"It would do no good. Keep your letters to yourself. I have seen many such documents."

"Now, Dr. W., all I ask for is that you give me the chance to prove to you that I am an honest man, for I feel badly hurt by your words."

"Do not trouble yourself about that. At any rate, I am sorry I can do nothing for you. Good-night, sir!"

The unexpected assault upon my integrity and veracity intensified the darkness of the night into which I plunged again, wounded to the heart. It was distressing enough to be homeless, weary, and in want; but to be accused of being a swindler seemed to overshadow all other trials. But hope triumphed over despair and pointed me to the best which was yet to be. I returned to the railway station with the intention of spending the night there. But the ticket agent thought differently. His "orders" required him to lock the doors of the station at a certain hour in the night, leaving no transient lodgers inside. I moved from the station to the park and stretched my weary mortal coil on one of the benches. The air was balmy, and I had as good a pillow (the iron arm of the bench) as my countryman of old, Jacob, had at Peniel. There I would spend the night under the beneficent heavens, meditating while awake upon the time when I should close the doors of some great university behind me, departing not thence until I had become a full-fledged scholar.

At about midnight, the sequel of the balmy air which enabled me to sleep in the park comfortably without extra covering arrived. The heavens wept over me large generous tears which drove me to a pretentious hotel near by, where the "night clerk" met me in a stern, businesslike manner and most cruelly charged me fifty cents for half a night's lodging in the cheapest room he had.

In my Arabic diary of that period, under date of December 29, 1893, I find the following entry which shows what impressions that eventful year left on me, and indicates also my turn of mind and hope for the future:—

"I shall always remember the events of 1893 as distressing and full of bitter pain. At times I really longed for death and loved it. Many were my difficulties and trials, and I had no home where to rest and no real friends to whom to unburden my heart. But God has mysterious purposes beyond our power to know. He has sustained me and led me safely through all my difficulties. It is good that I have been taught by my distresses to better appreciate the comforts of life. Now there is light on my pathway, and I see myself moving steadily toward better things. My hope that the Most High is leading me to that which He knows is best for me and pleasing to Him grows stronger from day to day, and I shall yet reach my goal, by his help, and preach to the world his pure and undefiled religion."

Yes, life's smiles are, on the whole, much more numerous than its frowns, and, notwithstanding all its afflictions, this world is keyed to goodness. My first appearance before an American audience occurred at New Brighton, Pennsylvania, where, if I remember correctly, a minister of the United Presbyterian Church permitted me to speak on the Holy Land at his prayer-meeting. As the meeting (which was not of the ordinary drowsy type) progressed, my whole soul said, "Lord, it is good to be here." The minister, who was past middle age and wore a most benignant countenance, conducted the service with such simple dignity and sweetness of spirit that the whole scene was transformed into a benediction. His lesson was from Acts XII, the story of Peter's miraculous release from prison. I shall never forget the sweet, informing, and persuasive modulations of that preacher's voice as he sought to show that although the band of Christians who were gathered together at the house of Mary, the mother of John, were praying for the release of the imprisoned apostle, yet when they were told by the damsel, Rhoda, that Peter stood at the door, they were afraid to open and receive the answer to their prayer. "They prayed God to bring Peter to them," said the preacher. "God did bring the apostle to the door, but those praying Christians were afraid to open and say, 'Come in!'"

I have never been able to ascertain the initial cause of my decision to enter the ministry, nor to point to the exact time when I was "called" to it. What I am certain of, however, is that the influences of such occasions as the one mentioned above did more than any others I know to lead me to the pulpit. It was the virile and irresistible leaven of the characters of those Christians of the various denominations, who did not so much profess correct creeds as reflect the life of the Master in their own lives, which led me in a mysterious way to add to my decision to enter college the decision to make my life-work the holy ministry of religion.

When I stood up to address the meeting, the cordial, sympathetic attitude of the audience soon calmed the violent beating of my heart

RAILWAY STATION, ELYRIA, OHIO

Where Mr. Rihbany was not allowed to spend the night

and stopped the knocking of my knees together, but it had no appreciable effect on my grammar and diction. The nouns and the verbs often stood at cross-purposes in my remarks, and the adjectives and adverbs interchanged positions, regardless of consequences. My impromptu literal translation of Arabic into English greatly puzzled the minds of my hearers, and, at times, it was difficult even for me to know fully what I was saying or wanted to say. Notwithstanding all that, however, I managed in closing to shift from Syria to America and eulogize George Washington. The minister asked for a contribution for me to help me go to college. As my engagement to speak had not been made known to my hearers before they came to the meeting, many of them were unprepared to give; the contribution was therefore small, but the meeting was rich in good things, and I went away in a happy and optimistic frame of mind.

If any one had told me on that evening in New Brighton that less than three years later I was to become the regular minister of an

American congregation and a "stump speaker"
in favor of the "gold standard," I should have
considered him a very flighty day-dreamer.
But America, the mother of modern wonders,
began to reveal itself to me and in me. I soon
became possessed by the consciousness that the
whole country was a vast university which
offered a thousand incentives to progress; that
I had the privilege of being born again in a land
which more than any other on our planet estab-
lishes the truth of the New Testament promise,
"Ask, and it shall be given you; seek, and ye
shall find; knock, and it shall be opened unto
you."

The Oriental, as a rule, lives his life in a general way, allowing a large portion of its area
to remain rather chaotic. The American lives
his life in detail, with order as its basic princi-
ple. I was very curious to know, after leaving
New York and Pittsburg, how the smaller
towns of America would impress me. Were
they as insignificant and as wanting in enterprise and culture compared with those large

cities, as the Syrian towns compared with Beyrout and Damascus? I was rapturously amazed to find every small city and town to be New York on a smaller scale. Each town had its "Main Street" and "Washington Street" and many other streets. Each town had its town hall, post-office, banks, newspapers, schools, and churches. And, oh, the home libraries, the musical instruments, the pictures on the walls, the "striking" clocks, and, above all, that idealism which makes the American woman, after doing her housework, "dress up for the afternoon," dash a little powder on her nose, and turn to her books or her piano. Certainly, such a nation is not "sunk deep in crass materialism."

I was told while in Syria that in America money could be picked up everywhere. That was not true. But I found that infinitely better things than money — knowledge, freedom, self-reliance, order, cleanliness, sovereign human rights, self-government, and all that these great accomplishments imply — can be picked up everywhere in America by whosoever earnestly seeks them. And those among Americans who are exerting the largest influence toward the solution of the "immigration problem" are, in my opinion, not those who are writing books on "good citizenship," but those who stand before the foreigner as the embodiment of these great ideals.

The occasions on which I was made to feel that I was a foreigner — an alien — were so rare that they are not worth mentioning. My purpose in life, and the large warm heart of America which opens wide to every person who aspires to be a good and useful citizen, made me forget that there was an "immigration problem" within the borders of this great Commonwealth. When I think of the thousand noble impulses which were poured into my soul in my early years in this country by good men and women in all the walks of life; when I think of the many homes in which I was received with my uncomely appearance and with my crude manners, where women who were visions of elegance served me as an honored guest, of the many counsels of men of affairs which fed my strength and taught me the lasting value of personal achievements, and that America is the land of, not only great privileges, but great responsibilities, I feel like saying (and I do say whenever I have the opportunity) to every foreigner, "When you really know what America is, when you are willing to share in its sorrows, as well as its joys, then you will cease to be a whining malcontent, will take your harp down from the willows, and will not call such a country 'a strange land.'"

Of all the means of improvement other than personal associations with good men and women, the churches and the public schools gripped most strongly at the strings of my heart. Upon coming into town, the sight of the church spires rising above the houses and the trees as witnesses to man's desire for God, always gave me inward delight. True, religion in America lacks to a certain extent the depth of Oriental mysticism; yet it is much more closely related than in the Orient to the vital issues of "the life which now is." Often would I go and stand on the opposite side of the street from a public-school building at the hour of dismissal (and this passion still remains with me) just for the purpose of feasting my eyes on seeing the pupils pour out in squads, so clean and so orderly, and seemingly animated by all that is noblest in the life of this great nation. My soul would revel in the thought that no distinctions were made in those temples of learning between Jew and Gentile, Protestant and Catholic, the churched and the unchurched; all enjoyed the equality of privilege, shared equally in the intellectual and moral feast, and drank freely the spirit of the noblest patriotism.

My progress in the English language was as surprising to me as it was delightful. When I first met Edward Everett Hale in Boston, in 1903, the first thing he said to me when I slipped my hand into his ponderous palm was, "How in the world have you managed to speak English so well?"

"I do not know," was my answer.

I really did not. It is wonderful what even a few months can do to equip with linguistic facilities a person who listens with his ears and his understanding alike. The vocabulary of every succeeding day shames that of the day before. My being entirely cut off from using the Arabic language was my greatest aid in acquiring English. My vocabulary, which has become varied and flexible enough for my purposes, was not acquired from a forced study of the classics. It poured into me from the lips of living men in all the walks of life. I listened with eager sympathy to the words of preachers, merchants, artisans, farmers, hack-drivers, housewives, and others who spoke as they *felt* in dealing with the various issues of life.

I owe a great debt to the live language of the English Bible. On occasions, I would open my Arabic Bible at church and follow the Scripture lesson as read by the minister, and thus learn what the English words meant. On other occasions, I would open my English Bible and learn how the words were pronounced. Thus the English has come to me saturated and mellowed with feeling. The phrases of the English Bible are elemental human sentiments made tangible.

It was in Chillicothe, Ohio, that I had my first glimpse into American history. The "hard times" did not prevent me from buying "A Brief History of the United States," the contents of which I virtually devoured. My instructors were my fellow guests at a comfortable and respectable boarding-house. I would retire into my room, ponder the annals of this modern "chosen people" until I reached a passage whose words proved too big for my mind to grasp (which was often the case), when I would go out and demand light on the subject from the first guest I happened to meet. A physician's wife and the genial gray-haired proprietor of the boarding-house manifested deep interest in me and were ever ready to aid my strenuous endeavor to become "an enlightened American citizen."

The proprietor, who, I believe, had fought in

the Civil War, would relate to me events of that great conflict in such a droll manner that my study of history under his supervision was a supreme delight.

"Yes," he would say, "we did hang Jeff Davis on a sour-apple tree, or we would have done it but for our respectability. We whipped those fellows down there pretty soundly. We spanked them so hard that I am certain they never will do it again."

But the genial proprietor enlightened me on other subjects than that of the Civil War. He gave me my first real lesson in English on table-manners. One day he asked me, "How do you like our grub?" "What is your grub, sir?" I asked. With a mischievous smile which scarcely agitated his weeping-willow mustache and thick beard, he said, "It is the things we eat, you know. And — and — it is part of good manners to show — in — in — some way that we like the grub, just to please our host." That was to me a most welcome bit of information. I had been greatly at a loss to know how to express in the English language my appreciation of a good dinner. Certainly now I had no longer an excuse to omit such a cultured formality. It was only a short time thereafter that I happened to dine with a Lutheran minister whose gracious wife served for the occasion a bounteous and elegantly appointed dinner. I could hardly wait for the proper moment to express my great appreciation of the repast. When the moment came, I turned to my hostess with cheerful dignity and said, "Mrs. F., I have greatly enjoyed your grub." But when her husband laughed so that he fell from his chair, I suspected that my instruction in table-manners at Chillicothe was somewhat defective.

It was in the little town of Elmore, Ohio, in the early autumn of 1893, that I felt for the first time that I could hold the attention of an American audience. There I was permitted to address a union meeting of the churches in the Presbyterian Church on a Sunday evening. The little building was crowded to the doors. My subject was "Turkey and America Contrasted."

LIGHTS AND SHADOWS

I do not know what did it, but my auditors were so deeply moved that they interrupted me twice with loud and prolonged applause, regardless of the fact that the service was essentially religious, the time Sunday, and the place a Presbyterian Church. At the close of the meeting, the minister of the church with a cordial handshake reinforced my ambition with the generous prophecy, "My brother, whatever else you might, or might not, become, you are going to make a very effective public speaker. Keep right on."

Well, I am still keeping on.

It was in that little town also that I first heard "America" sung. The line "Land where my fathers died" stuck in my throat. I envied every person in that audience who could sing it truthfully. For years afterward, whenever I tried to sing those words, I seemed to myself to be an intruder. At last a new light broke upon my understanding. At last I was led to realize that the fathers of my new and higher self did live and die in America. I was born in Syria as a child, but I was born in America as a man.

All those who fought for the freedom I enjoy, for the civic ideals I cherish, for the simple but lofty virtues of the typical American home which I love, were *my fathers!* Therefore, I could sing the words "Land where my fathers died " with as much truth and justice as the words, "Land of the pilgrim's pride."

From Elmore I proceeded to Wauseon, Ohio, a town which numbered then about three thousand inhabitants, and where a new chapter was opened in my life's history. Upon my arrival in this town, I called on the Congregational minister, and, finding him willing to open his church for me to lecture, requested him to direct me to some "Christian boarding-house." The friendly divine conducted me to a private house where lived two widowed sisters who had room and time enough to care for a few of the "good class" of boarders. I was not long in that modest home before I discovered that the two ladies were lovers of good books and profoundly religious. Through the kinship of our spirits, and upon hearing my story and learning of my life's purpose, they became deeply interested in me. They said they seemed to perceive that I had "a bright and useful future" before me and they wished to share in its realization.

The two good sisters, Mrs. Susan Baldwin and Mrs. Rosa Kolb, were not rich in this world's goods. But they had a home, and, so long as I had none, I was most cordially invited to share that home with them as a younger brother. There I might return from my travels and find sympathetic friends ready to aid me, by their counsel and other friendly services, to conquer my difficulties and get nearer to my life's goal. In my wanderings up to that time, I had not lacked words of encouragement and inspiration which seemed to pour out from the heart of a nation whose spirit is friendliness and whose genius is progress. Notwithstanding all that, however, my being tossed about by every wind of difficulty while I had nowhere to lay my head, had begun to tell on me. Down beneath my conscious resolution a counter-current had set in. A keen yearning for friends and a fixed abode (which is strongest in the Oriental nature) would at intervals flood my soul with sadness. No doubt that friendly, though humble, home in Bethany furthered mightily the triumph of the Gospel.

The gracious, friendly offer of the two sisters came to me as a most timely reinforcement. When I think how my strength and courage were renewed and my cup of inspiration was refilled by their manifold and never-failing services to me, I realize most clearly that we do not need to be rich in order to be helpful, nor known to fame in order to be inspiring. I cannot contemplate what success I have achieved or might achieve in life without feeling that but for the influence of those two good women the story of my life might have been entirely different from what it is.

It was in the Congregational Church of Wauseon that I preached my first real sermon in America. After the manner of all youthful preachers, I chose a subject which might have staggered the powers of a Beecher or a Phillips

Brooks. My bold purpose was, first, to prove the existence of God; second, to show how the soul was related to Him; third, to persuade my hearers to believe that an irreligious person was only an animal, and had no eternal life in him. I had constructed my premises, drawn my conclusions, and planned my final assault in Arabic, and trusted the reproduction of all this formidable array of ideas, in English, to the "inspiration of the pulpit." I trust that my hearers still believed in God, notwithstanding all my toilsome, painful, and unintelligible efforts to prove his existence. The effect of the "sermon" was indicated to me at the close of the service by a remark which I overheard a lady make to another. "Poor fellow," said the charitable woman, "in all probability he had an idea, but certainly not the language to express it."

Nor did I fare better four years later when I preached again in that same church, after I had been the regular pastor of a church for more than a year, and had been told that I did preach acceptable sermons. On this occasion, while walking home with a friend after the service, he turned to me, and, with a mischievous smile, said, "Do you remember, when about four years ago you preached here, that it was said you probably had an idea, but not the words to express it?" "Yes," I answered, expecting a veritable psalm of praise for my later achievement. "Well," he said, "this morning it was *just the reverse!* "

It was while at my newly found home in Wauseon that I first became deeply interested in the history of the Civil War, and began to see clearly what this country, which we newcomers found ready for us with all its unparalleled privileges, cost in blood and treasure to preserve its unity and guard its institutions. My soul was fired with admiration for the devotion, heroism, and endurance of the American volunteer soldier, of both the North and the South. And, oh, the story of Abraham Lincoln! How it opened every vein of sympathy in my nature and awakened in me deep, almost religious reverence for the memory of that "rich and various man." As I read and re-read the records of his journey from a log cabin to the White House, Lincoln seemed to me to be the noblest human example this side the Crucifixion, and the supreme vindication of democracy.

And now to say that my enthusiasm for the martyr president has been sobered down and relieved of its high coloring, does by no means indicate a reversal of my youthful estimate of his worth. No; Abraham Lincoln remains to me as one of the great world-builders and saviors of humanity. But my present opinion is that, if humanity is not to be pronounced a failure, no one individual can be so good above all other individuals, nor of sufficiently inclusive greatness as to be called the noblest human example and the supreme vindication of democracy. I find the vindication of democracy not only in the career of Lincoln, but also in the million men who left their occupations and responded to his call to arms to defend a national ideal; I find it in the fortitude and sacrificing love of the countless American mothers, wives, and sisters, who bade their men go forth and give their fullest measure of devotion to the homes and altars of their country. I find the supreme vindication of democracy in this nation's survival of the shocks of the greatest civil war in history; in that great historic triumph of reason over the passions in a reunited North and South; in America's millions of happy homes; in its multitudes of schools and libraries, which are "free to all," and in the fact that its power of cohesion is neither that of standing armies, nor yet of superimposed laws, but the intelligence of its citizens and mutual good will among them. I find the vindication of democracy in the marvelous assimilative powers of America through which hosts of aliens are enfranchised in peace and freedom, intellectually, politically, and socially; in the fact that one may travel through the whole vast territory called the United States, the home of a hundred million souls, without encountering a custom-house, a "frontier guard," or a constabulary squad; in the American citizen's love for fair play and his deep conviction that right only makes might.

In the State of Indiana I first came into close touch with the well-known religious "revivals," and formed a clear idea of what Protestantism calls "conversion." I was deeply impressed by the zeal with which the Christians labored to bring "sinners" to Christ, and the fact that during a revival the religious idea loomed highest in the community. But I must say it was not long before I developed a decided dislike to the methods of professional "Evangelists," whose message contained infinitely more fear of hell-fire than love for the Christ-life, and to whom the clearest evidence of the religious interest in a community was the size of the collection.

One of my first experiences (and it was rather grim) at a revival took place in the town of Kokomo, Indiana. The meetings were being held in a Methodist church, but I am not certain whether it was the regular Methodists or some other branch. Toward the close of the meeting, which I attended, tearful sentiments converted the service into a veritable Babel. Presently a woman who, as I was told later "got the power," sprang up from her seat and, shouting, "Glory to Jesus!" dashed about, embracing whosoever came in her way. I remained reasonably collected until I saw her heading for me with open arms. Just think of a Syrian youth with all his psychological antecedents with regard to woman, in such a situation! I instantly decided that I would not be embraced, even though the motive of my pursuer was purely spiritual. I slipped precipitately behind a large pillar; the lady, seemingly not particular whom she embraced, bestowed her affections on more courageous worshipers, while I effected my escape. I never returned to those meetings.

In contrast with the above experience, I will relate another I had in Columbia City of the same State. Through the kindness of its minister, I was permitted to mount the pulpit of the Presbyterian Church on a Sunday morning and give a talk on Syria. I spied in the audience a gentleman of a penetrating but kindly eye who seemed to listen with rapt attention. The next morning the minister of the church told me that a gentleman who had heard me the day before wished to see me at his office; that he was a lawyer and a "fine gentleman" by the name of Marshall. The minister went with me to the law office, introduced me to the gentleman, whom I recognized as the good listener I had seen at the church, and departed, leaving us alone. Mr. Marshall asked me a few questions about my birthplace and my plans for the future, and I answered that my plans were to become a good American citizen, and, if possible, a preacher. He smiled in a very genial manner, and, reaching into his pocket, handed me a five-dollar bill as his contribution which he was not prepared to give at the Sunday service, saying, "I am sure you will make good use of it." The years passed, and, while I often thought of that good Mr. Marshall, I lost connection with him until 1912, when Mr. Thomas R. Marshall was nominated for Vice-President of the United States and later elected. The appearance of his picture in the newspapers, and the fact that he practiced law in Columbia City in 1893, brought me again in touch with my benefactor.

CHAPTER XII

COLLEGE AND PULPIT

BUT I have still more — much more — to say about Indiana. Late in the winter of 1894, I happened to be in the small town of Butler in the Hoosier State, where I delivered two addresses. One of my hearers, the principal of the schools, became deeply interested in me "at first sight" and made me an offer right then and there which made me wildly interested in him. Mr. K.'s entrancing story was this. An anonymous philanthropist had placed at his disposal one million dollars as an endowment for a small college. The high purpose of the donor was not only to equip such a college with every modern educational facility, and thus make it rival the great universities, but that no promising young man who sought to enter this institution, especially if his goal were the ministry, should be turned out for lack of funds.

What seemed obvious to Mr. K., and even I

could see it, was that my case came most snugly within the purpose of the donor. I was "promising," I lacked funds, my goal was the ministry. Therefore, all my fretting and worrying about securing a college education should now cease. Furthermore, being a stranger in a strange land, I was to enjoy the personal attention and friendship of Mr. K., who, according to the terms of the endowment, was to be the president of the college. I was to be provided with everything I needed as a student, in return for which favors I was to deliver a certain number of lectures (dates to be made by the president) every year in various parts of the state and thus advertise the college. The prospective president further informed me that he was about to secure control of a small college at North Manchester, Indiana, of which he expected to take actual possession in the following September and transform it so as to fit the plans of the hidden millionaire.

While Mr. K. was unfolding his proposition, streaks of lightning ran up and down my spine.

I felt as if I were in a dream of sanctifying beauty, and was afraid to move even a muscle for fear of waking up and losing the vision. At last, college! All my pain and sorrow, hunger and fatigue, were about to be transfigured into glorious victories; my prayers were to be answered and my highest hopes fulfilled. Could it be true? College? And on such terms! A million dollars back of me and the president of the college my personal friend. It was difficult for me not to believe that in some way I was a millionaire myself. Somehow I managed to break the enthralling spell of the occasion enough to thank Mr. K. with genuine Oriental effusiveness for his surpassing kindness, and to promise most solemnly to be at North Manchester College on the 4th day of the following September.

From the time I met Mr. K., in the latter part of February, 1894, until September of the same year, when I was to enter college as an especially favored student, my whole life was a state of intense expectancy. The future so beamed with joy that, like a child on Christmas Eve, I often wished I might have fallen asleep at the end of our conversation and awakened in the classroom at the college.

In the mean time, my friend Mr. K. was leading to a successful conclusion negotiations to secure control of the small college at North Manchester, Indiana. Finally, the college, which had been struggling painfully for years to maintain its existence, was placed in his hands, and he proceeded with characteristic Western enterprise to mature the plans stipulated in the endowment contract.

On the 4th day of September, 1894, my pilgrim staff rested in North Manchester. There I found Mr. K. bearing the prerogatives of his office as college president with the simple dignity of a Lincoln. The citizens were happy that a new and virile educational era was dawning upon their town. A corps of efficient professors took charge of the various departments, and a happy student body, numbering about two hundred, sought the pabulum of knowledge at the richly endowed institution. Those of us who were to receive special financial aid were known as the millionaire students, which designation we bore with becoming dignity. But there were other especially favored students. One of Mr. K.'s schemes, which seemed to him to mark an advance in the history of education, was that every student who secured five other pay students should be given a free scholarship, a privilege of which a few enterprising students availed themselves. Literary societies, political clubs, and prayer circles were soon organized, and all signs inspired the hope that ere long our college would merit the title of the "Harvard of the Middle West."

The theological department, in which I was especially interested, was under the sole control of an elderly preacher who succeeded eminently in convincing his pupils that he knew Hebrew, Greek, and Latin. He was a devout man, brimful of friendliness and fatherly counsel. Perhaps his most serious defect was his strong tendency to doze during recitations.

On one occasion, in order to awaken him in a polite manner, we sang a hymn. He woke and was so pleased with our melody that he discoursed to us for about half an hour on the power of music over a congregation.

My life in North Manchester was most happy. American friendliness and hospitality never seemed to me to be more free and abundant than in that little city. The demand for me as a lecturer and preacher was always more than I could supply. On one occasion I was highly honored by being asked to represent the college at a patriotic celebration and make an address on George Washington. I took for my text the story of the hatchet, and proved conclusively that the Father of his Country was a very honest man, concluding with the admonition that, in order to be worthy of such a father, as American citizens we should all be honest.

The entire population of the college, as well as the town, had implicit faith in the "anonymous millionaire" until the beginning of the second term, when the treasurer of the college, having spent all the tuition money he had received at the beginning of the school year, became suddenly insolvent. He was in frequent consultation with the president, when attitudes spoke louder than words. The countenances of our poor professors began to betray a portentous situation, and the student body was seized with a secret fear such as is felt upon the first intimations of an earthquake. At last the treasurer became more communicative and informed the faculty that the college was in "financial straits." "What? With a million dollars back of it?" When appealed to for funds, the president stated rather cheerfully that *ultimately* all was safe. The reason, he said, that the "millionaire" had not yet turned over to the college treasurer the first installment of the endowment fund was due to the fact that the citizens of the town had not as yet met the terms of their agreement by beginning the erection of a certain building for the college. The citizens protested that they had never entered into such an agreement, but that they were willing to aid the college in every possible way, provided that a committee chosen from among their most highly respected citizens be permitted to meet the "donor" himself and ascertain his wishes with regard to what was expected of them. But the president contended that to reveal even the name of his wealthy friend would be base treachery on his part, adding emphatically that he would rather resign than commit such a deed.

"Some one had blundered," and thus what seemed, at least to Mr. K. and to me, one of the most significant educational enterprises of the nineteenth century, was practically killed in its infancy, just because a millionaire philanthropist insisted on interpreting literally the scriptural injunction, "When thou doest thine alms, let not thy left hand know what thy right hand doeth, that thine alms may be in secret." Just because of such a technicality, we, millionaire students, were suddenly reduced to pauperism.

The real secret of the "millionaire philan-

thropist" scheme in connection with North
Manchester College will probably remain forever the exclusive possession of Mr. K.'s soul.
Others' judgments of his case were various.
Some thought he was an innocent self-deceived
visionary; others concluded that he was a delib-
erate deceiver; others thought that he had been
made sport of by a sharper, who pretended to
be a millionaire. But what seemed most probable to many was that Mr. K. had thought that
his plan of giving a free scholarship to every
student who secured five other pay students
would insure for the college a sufficiently large
patronage to carry it through, and that he had
invented the millionaire myth as an incentive
to the trustees to place the struggling college
in his hands, on the theory that the end justi-
fied the means.

Whatever the original design of Mr. K. was,
I thanked him for his many kindnesses to me
and faced again my college problem, saying to
myself, "Wait on the Lord; be of good courage."

My few months of college life in North Manchester were not unfruitful of good things. My close contact with individuals and families in a typical American town deepened my insight into the life of a country my love for which had already become a ruling passion. Within the college I enjoyed the excellent opportunity of observing the various moods of American youth, from the political, social, and religious points of view. The few regular lessons I had were not without their guiding influence toward systematic thinking; my vocabulary was greatly enriched and my self-confidence as a public speaker much strengthened. And not the least of the results of my brief career as a "millionaire student" was the following smile of Fortune.

During my last week in the ill-starred college, I met a Methodist minister of Des Moines, Iowa, the Reverend W. A. Wiseman, whose three children were among our students. Mr. Wiseman said to me in a very gracious, complimentary manner that, two days before, he had heard me give a lecture on the Orient, with some observations on American life, which not only deeply interested him, but convinced him that I had a message which the general public needed to hear. Furthermore, he said that he was in deep sympathy with my purpose to secure a college education and enter the ministry. Therefore, if the offer met my approval, he would like to be my "advance agent" and plan for me a regular "lecture tour" in the Farther West, which would bring me more money than any lecturing for a "collection" could. His final proposition was that he would give me two hundred dollars and pay all my expenses for twenty-four consecutive dates. He explained that since I was not known to fame, he could not ask a higher price for a lecture than twenty or twenty-five dollars, and that, by the time he had paid all my expenses, the cost of advertising and other incidentals, his share of the proceeds would be much smaller than mine.

Of course, two hundred dollars had not the hypnotic charm of a million, but it was the biggest sum of *real* money I had ever fancied my lecturing would bring me in one month. I did not allow Mr. Wiseman to leave my room before I closed the contract with him.

My lecturing tour began in the city of Des Moines, most auspiciously. A large and appreciative audience gave me a most cordial reception. The "Iowa State Register" published, the following day, this report (in all probability written by Mr. Wiseman): "Mr. A. M. Rihbany, a native of the Holy Land, lectured at Grace M. E. Church last night to a large and delighted audience. He is a speaker of great ability and keeps his audience in fine humor from beginning to end. No lecture given in Grace Church ever gave such universal satisfaction." That was all that was necessary for us to "sweep" the State of Iowa and a considerable portion of Illinois. Prosperity and joy attended our course, at the end of which I found in my possession, for the first time, two hundred dollars in real "greenbacks." Certainly now not all the Fates could prevent me from securing a college education.

Early in September, 1895, I matriculated at

the Ohio Wesleyan University. My fear that I might not be able to complete the regular course led me to elect a special course. I chose my studies as a boy picks apples out of a basket — taking the biggest. All but one of the branches I elected came in the Junior and Senior years. To the protest of the president that such studies were too advanced for me, I answered most conceitedly that I should be very willing to take less advanced studies if I failed to measure up to the other students in those higher classes. I was permitted to follow the course I had chosen. The compassion of my professors, coupled with some effort on my part, prevented me from being transferred to the lower classes.

The Ohio Wesleyan University of that period was suffering from that affliction which was, and to a large extent still is, common to denominational institutions. As a rule, its professors were chosen not so much with reference to their qualifications as instructors and educators, as to their doctrinal "soundness." Consequently the university was heavily over-preached.

The surplus of doctrinal soundness could not be used to make up the deficit occurring on the educational side. But the branches in which I was deeply interested — psychology, ethics, history, and English literature — were taught by two professors who were considered the most modern and efficient in the entire institution, and the pioneers of a new era of ampler educational facilities and greater usefulness, which the university now enjoys. They had "a vital touch to them," and their methods stimulated thought and encouraged independent research.

At the end of my second term in college, I became again "financially embarrassed." In view of the fact that among the eight hundred students there were many "local preachers" who were endeavoring to make their way through college by preaching in the churches for miles around, my opportunities for lecturing and preaching were greatly limited. Was it not, therefore, the part of wisdom for me to leave college for a time and reënter the lecture field

UNIVERSITY HALL AND GREY CHAPEL, OHIO WESLEYAN UNIVERSITY

with my friend Mr. Wiseman, secure the necessary funds, and return to the university the following September? So it seemed to me and to my good professors, who, while regretting the emergency which made such a course necessary, earnestly hoped for my return to them in the autumn.

And here I wish to quote a generous message which came to me from my professor in history (whom I have not seen since I left college) at the conclusion of my series of articles in the "Atlantic Monthly": —

DELAWARE, OHIO,
March 26, 1914.

DEAR SIR AND BROTHER, — Your articles in the "Atlantic Monthly" have been much enjoyed in our home. The name had a familiar sound to me, yet I did not trace its familiarity until in the last "Atlantic" I read that you were in the Ohio Wesleyan University in 1895. This led me to look up the class-rolls of that term, the fall, and there I found your name in the list of a goodly class which was at work upon the Middle Ages. I also noticed that your grade was one of the best in the class.

What a fine thing it is for you, a stranger, to give such lessons of grateful appreciation of the free air of America to many of our young people who, I fear, do not know to what they have been born. Let me thank you for what you have said to them in so bright and attractive a fashion, not alloyed with pessimism, but radiant with real faith in God and man. May you have great good for your portion. The Ohio Wesleyan University is trying to do her best for this generation.

With best wishes and appreciation,

Sincerely yours,

R. T. STEVENSON.

When, about the middle of March, 1896, I left the Ohio Wesleyan University for the little town of Morenci, Michigan, where my friends had moved from Wauseon, Ohio, and where I was destined to live for several years, I little dreamed that I should never see a college again as a student. In April and May I "toured the West" again as a lecturer, and again in August. Shortly after my return to Morenci, the Methodist minister called on me on a Friday evening and requested me to preach in his stead at a union meeting of all the churches of the town, to be held in the Congregational Church on the following Sunday evening. The time for preparation was short, but the request was urgent and I consented to serve. In my brief diary of that year, written in Arabic, I find the following entry, literally translated: "Saturday, September 5 — Spent the greater part of this day in preparing myself for a sermon which I will preach in the Congregational Church here at a general (union) meeting."

On the following Sunday evening a large audience taxed the capacity of the Congregational Church. My text was from Luke XII, 48: "To whomsoever much is given, of him shall much be required." The cordial eagerness of my auditors was inspiring, and I spoke from the depth of my soul.

At the close of the service many of my hearers were most generous with their appreciative remarks; as typical Americans they believed in encouraging a beginner, in "helping a fellow along." But my sermon on that evening brought to me other significant and utterly unexpected results. During the following week the senior deacon of the Congregational Church came to me with the following, to me most astonishing, proposition. "Our people," he said, "were so pleased with your sermon last Sunday night that they have directed me to ask you if you would not take charge of our pulpit for the coming winter and become our regular pastor." For the moment I could not believe that the good man was really serious in what he said. "I to become your regular pastor?" was my astonished question to him. "Yes, if you will," he replied with a very genial smile.

To my objection on the ground that my English was as yet barbarous, and utterly unfit for devotional services; that I had not had a college or theological education, and had not the slightest knowledge of pastoral duties, he replied to the effect that colleges did not really make preachers; that although I did at times split the infinitive and use an adjective where an adverb should have been used, all such matters were of small importance. "There is something vital in your utterances," he added, "and it is that something which we are after. Your emphasizing the wrong word or syllable now and then gives your message a pleasant flavor. As to pastoral duties, you will learn them as you go."

Notwithstanding the fact that the gracious words of the deacon greatly expanded my youthful vanity, I did not feel vain enough to accept the offer. I consented, however, to supply the pulpit of the Congregational Church for a few Sundays before going West on another lecturing tour. So I did. But upon my return from the West, those good Congregationalists renewed their offer to me with greater insistence and cordiality, and again I consented only to supply their pulpit for a season.

But, on this occasion, I urged another objection to my becoming the regular pastor of a church. About that time the entire country was on fire with political excitement. The campaign of 1896, one of the most agitating, most spectacular campaigns in the history of America, was upon us, and, as a true patriot, fired with the zeal of a new convert, I decided to remain free from the limitations of a ministerial position in order that I might "serve my country politically." I would first do my utmost to save the nation from the "disgrace and ultimate ruin of cheap money." Bimetallism, "sixteen-to-one," the double standard, and other heresies, seemed to me to be like smallpox, cancer, and diphtheria, which must be stamped out at whatever cost. I would preach on Sundays to the best of my ability under the circumstances, but on all other days I would place myself on the altar of the "Gold Standard," the savior of the commercial integrity of the nation.

I devoted myself unreservedly to the study of

the monetary question. You might not think that my sources — campaign documents — were the most reliable, but they were the only means at hand, and the time was short. Besides, they had been published by Republicans whose learning and veracity I had no reason to suspect — chiefly because the Republican party had "saved the Union" in 1861–65, long before I was born.

I did make several speeches which met with the heartiest approval of my fellow citizens — the Republicans. One of them, an influential leader in local politics, said to me one day, "You can't convince me that you had never studied the monetary problem before this campaign. You must have studied it in Europe or somewhere else. I have learned more from you on the present issue than from those 'big guns' that the State Central Committee sends to us. You ought to head for the Legislature instead of the pulpit. Do let us start the 'boom' for the next state campaign."

The suggested "boom" had no attraction for

me. My goal was the pulpit. But I was decidedly proud of what I did in that great campaign. No king, I believe, ever felt more exalted with his crown and scepter than I did whenever I said "My country!" Just think of me, the child of ages of oppression, now having a great country to serve, to defend, nay, to *save* from impending ruin! It was undefiled glory to address "my fellow citizens," even to carry a torch — a lighted one — and join the procession under the Stars and Stripes.

The country having been "saved" at the election, I turned my undivided attention again to the ministry. The Congregationalists of Morenci were still waiting for me with the attractive offer to become their pastor; my relations with them had been growing more pleasant as time passed, and, after much hesitation and with some misgivings as to my fitness for the position, I accepted the "call" and postponed indefinitely the matter of my return to college.

It may not be uninteresting to the reader to

FIRST CONGREGATIONAL CHURCH, MORENCI, MICHIGAN

know that I did not come into the office of a
pastor alone. The romance of "love at first
sight" had already occurred; Cupid's arrows,
which no barriers of race or language can
check, had already pierced two hearts, the one
Semitic, the other Aryan, and made them bleed
for one another. The sacred union, which the
Church blesses and the State makes legal, followed, and brought to my side an American
wife from Ohio to share with me the trials and
triumphs of the ministry. And it may interest
the reader to know also that notwithstanding
the fact that, in reporting this marriage, the
editor of the "Ohio State Journal" used the
heading, "An Ohio School Teacher Has Poor
Taste," I have already forgiven him, for he
knew not what he did — he never saw me.

Now before undertaking to write concerning
the Gospel which I felt commissioned to preach
when I assumed the office of a Christian minister, I wish to mention an event which bears a
very close relation to my political activities.
When war between this country and Spain

seemed inevitable, I decided that if the circumstances required I would enlist, not as a chaplain, but as a private soldier. Consequently I wrote to my father with regard to the matter, begging not only his opinion but his consent. Having in mind the warlike spirit of the Rihbany clan, I was not very greatly astonished when I received the following letter: —

BETATER, LEBANON, SYRIA.

To our Beloved and Honored Son, may God protect him: —

We send you our intense love and parental blessings from the depth of our hearts which are deeply wounded for your absence, for you are the possessor of our hearts in life and in death. We ask daily the mighty God to bless you and keep you and multiply the fruits of the labor of your hands. Your letter is received and we thank God that you and your honorable wife are safe and well. We learn from your letter that there is war between your government and that of Spain and that you intend to enlist if needed. This news causes us intense anxiety and life seems worthless without you. Nevertheless, O dear son, such being the case, we commit you to God, hoping that His mighty arm may protect you. First we ask that God may bring peace on earth; and second we beseech you, O our son, not to shrink from entering the army to fight for your government. We know that you are brave, and bravery is characteristic of your clan and ancestors. As long as you are an American citizen, you must fight for your exalted government, and not only you, but if your brothers can help fight your enemies we would gladly send them over to America. America has done much for you, and you ought to pay her back by fighting her enemies as an honorable man. We hope to see your luminous, smiling face again, but let us say, under the circumstances, "God's will be done." Your mother sends a thousand kisses to you and your wife. The Reverend Father, our priest Michael, sends also his rich blessing.

May God prolong your days.

YOUR FATHER.

Here I had not only my father's consent, but his mandate, to enlist. But Spain was considerate enough to give up the fight before I deemed it necessary to don the "blue."

CHAPTER XIII

AT THE TEMPLE GATE

When I first came into the pulpit as a regular minister, I was granted a salary of six hundred dollars a year and a "donation" — that is, the proceeds of an annual church supper at which the guests were supposed to pay more than the repast was worth. The success of the donation depended largely on the weather. I was simply a layman in earnest. The conventional phraseology of the pulpit was well-nigh unknown to me. I prayed at the sacred desk as simply as in my secret chamber, and preached in an unaffected conversational tone.

As has been already indicated, I had had no college education, no familiarity with authoritative systems of theology, and no extensive memories of creeds and catechisms. I was supremely conscious of one great fact, namely, that by my sincere and reverential consent to serve in the office of a Christian minister, I was ordained to preach the Gospel of Christ in the simplicity of the New Testament and not necessarily as it has been restated by any group of theologians. This attitude toward the ministerial office was the cumulative result of all my religious past.

Having departed from the Greek Church in my youth, I carried away with me from that fold not doctrines, but religious feelings. My Mother Church exerted upon me unconscious, mystic, indefinable spiritual influences. In the almost entire absence of preaching in that church doctrines are only implied in the ritual, not directly taught to the laity. As a Greek Orthodox, I simply took it for granted that the tenets of the faith of my church were absolutely correct.

When I first came in contact with Protestantism in the American mission school at Sûk-el-Gharb, that faith appealed to me as a more stimulating, more enlightened, and more enlightening form of the Christian religion than the one into which I was born. It was the intellectual and ethical phases of Protestantism which drew me away from the less reflective faith of my fathers. True, here I was taught doctrine, but always with the understanding that Protestantism was the Christianity of the open Bible, the individual conscience and private interpretation. Consequently, in that early period of my religious history, whenever I glanced over the scroll of my destiny, and in so far as I was able to do so, I thought of myself as a *free man in Christ*.

When I left my father's house in far-off Lebanon and came to the New World to struggle and to suffer, it was not the learned polemics and authoritative creeds of theologians which kept my heart from breaking. It was God, the compassionate Father, and Christ, the triumphant fellow-sufferer, who said to me, "Fear not, be not dismayed." It was He who loves us more than a mother loves her babe who walked with me the rough road of hunger and nakedness and loneliness, and was with me in the musty darkness of the tenement houses of New York, as a strengthening and consoling presence.

In my travels in this country before I entered the pulpit I studied Christianity not in catechisms but in the faces and characters and helpful deeds of living men and women of all creeds and no creed. I never knew the exact doctrinal positions of such persons. What I was aware of was that by their reverential and friendly attitude toward God and man, by the sanctity of their lives and their readiness to aid every good endeavor, such men and women addressed themselves to my inmost soul as fresh revelations of the divine spirit and as inspiring examples of the Christ-life.

Now, do you suppose that when I came into the pulpit to break the bread of life to my congregation, I was going to close my eyes to all these open visions of the spiritual life, my Protestant freedom and the simplicity of the New Testament, and turn to dusty and musty theological documents to find my faith, my God, and my Christ? To do so seemed to me to be like forsaking my newly acquired freedom as an American citizen and returning to the bondage of Turkish rule. No; as God revealed himself to Isaiah and Paul, so He reveals himself to me and to every soul that seeks Him. The Council of Nicæa, or any other council, had no more right to make an authoritative and infallible creed for the succeeding generations than it had the right to make an infallible bill of fare for every age and race.

With such ideas and convictions as my background, I preached to my people with the utmost directness and sincerity of which I was capable. My hearers often told me that I did not preach "after the usual manner," to which I answered that I did not know what the "usual manner" was. We loved one another. Our church prospered to the extent that we had to build an addition to our auditorium in order to accommodate our growing congregations and church activities.

During my ministry of nearly three years at Morenci, as I had no public library at hand and as I had but few books of my own, my reading was of necessity miscellaneous. My theological library consisted of two commentaries on the Bible: the one (written in the seventeenth century) given to me by a friend; the other (written in the eighteenth century) I bought from an enterprising publisher at a "slaughter sale of epoch-making books." Both of these commentaries are treasure-houses of preconceived ideas regarding God's attitude toward man and the universe. But during those years three books of quite different type fell into my hands. The first was "The Apostolic Age," by Professor A. C. McGiffert, concerning which, when I had read it, I concluded that its author believed in making use of his mental faculties and his reason even when writing "sacred history." The other two were "The Theology of Civilization," and "The Religion of a Gentleman," both by the Reverend Charles F. Dole, D.D., of Boston. These books convinced me not only that their author was a truly civilized man, but that he had succeeded in sounding the spiritual depths of human interrelations.

But my real book of theology was the New

Testament. I read it with the freedom with which the Master read the Old Testament in his day — as the freeman of the Spirit and not the bondman of the letter. I read it in my study, on trains, and in railway stations, with all my spiritual faculties alert, not so much to know what every single text meant as to discover the controlling purpose of the whole book.

It is indeed most difficult, if not impossible, to analyze the religious consciousness chronologically. But the fixing of dates and the defining of eras is not necessary here, because I am not writing a diary of events but trying to make a confession of faith. What I feel certain of is that no person can read the records of the spiritual life, as they are inscribed in the souls of well-meaning, kindly disposed men and women, and the New Testament, with reverent freedom, — taking into consideration the mentality and the social habits of the times and country in which it was written, — without feeling upborne by a spiritual tide high above all creeds and dogmas. It was such a state of mind of

which I became intensely conscious during my
second year in the pulpit. The words of the
Master, "Love the Lord thy God with all thy
heart, and thy neighbor as thyself," and, "On
these two commandments hang all the law and
the prophets," held undisputed sway over all
my thoughts and words. For me Christianity
shook itself free from all divisive dogmas and
appeared as the religion of brotherly love, of
trust and salvation, and not of fear and damnation. All good men of whatever creed or nationality seemed to me to be friends and disciples of Christ. In this frame of mind I could
not, of course, be an efficient helper at those
"revivals" at which professional "evangelists" consigned to hell the majority of mankind. A revival always seemed to me more like
a tragedy, poorly acted, than a profound spiritual experience. Whenever the evangelist would
compress the message and mission of Christ so
as to fit the narrow dimensions of his own particular view of Protestantism, and urge his
hearers (and by implication the world at large)

to believe or perish, my whole soul would say no. He who has taught us to forgive "seventy times seven," and to love our enemies, will not torture *his* enemies forever.

As all thoughts gravitate toward expression, and in view of the fact that I never intended to believe one thing and preach another, as time passed, my pulpit utterances became increasingly infected with liberalism. In proportion as the spiritual Christ prevailed with me over the dogmatic Christ, I felt the limitations of my theological environment and the suspicions of the conservatives in the community. My conception of my newly acquired freedom as priceless made me decidedly inhospitable to arbitrary restraints. When on one occasion one of my deacons advised me to keep my "broad views" to myself and preach the "accepted doctrines," I answered rather abruptly that I and my forefathers for centuries had suffered enough political and religious repression; that I had not learned my "broad views" at any heretical school. My teachers were Congregational Protestantism and Americanism, both of which urged me to "stand fast in the freedom wherewith Christ hath made us free."

Shortly after the close of the Spanish-American War, at the urgent invitation of my parents, who longed to "behold my face again before death parted us," and to "revive their hearts by beholding the Lady, my beloved American wife," I visited Syria. The people of Betater, both aristocrats and commoners, gave us a royal welcome. All the clans of the town called on us in fifties and hundreds. Invitations to feasts were more than we could accept. For the time being, the aristocrats admitted me into their ranks with cheerful generosity as "a man who had progressed much in the land of *effrenj*."

How did the old home appear to me after an absence of seven years? Well, from the pretentious buildings of Beyrout to the ordinary dwellings of Betater, everything seemed to me amazingly small. The scale of my vision had been so enlarged in giant America that upon

my arrival in Betater the place seemed to me
for all the world like a kindergarten. And what
was even more astonishing to me was my unconscious departure from many of the customs
of my people. The friendliness of the Syrians
is very inquisitive. It has very little regard for
what Americans call "private matters." On
the very evening of our arrival, old friends
assailed me with a multitude of questions which
could be answered only by the laying bare of
both my outer and inner worlds. One day an
acquaintance, whom I had forgotten altogether,
arrived at our home. He said to me that he had
journeyed two hours for the purpose of seeing
my "blessed face," and to inquire particularly
as to how much money I had — in all — and
how I managed to get an American wife. Of
course I was asked by many how old my American wife was, and whether the "clear color in
her face was *natural*." It required all the Yan-
kee shrewdness I had acquired in America to
evade such questions without giving offense.

But while on that memorable trip I saw again

Thabitah ("th" as in "three"), my first love, and the charmer of my childhood. Thabitah was the daughter of the owner of the double house into which our family was ushered on our arrival in Betater in 1875.

Her parents occupied one half of the house, and we the other half. Thabitah was born when I was about eight years old, and, after the custom of the country, I was made to believe by my parents and her parents that her "star" and my "star" were in "harmony"; therefore we were destined to marry one another. Real "matches" are made occasionally in Syria after this manner, but in the present case I was simply the victim of a joke. But being innocent of the frolicsome designs of our parents, I became deeply enamored of the black-eyed infant. No knight-errant was ever more ready to do the bidding of his lady than I was to do the errands which her mother asked me to do, and she was very free and generous in her demands. One day my mother missed me and went about searching for her lost boy.

After a long search in the neighborhood I was found fast sleep under Thabitah's old-fashioned cradle.

When I saw Thabitah again on my last visit to Syria she was on her way from the public oven (bakery). Her graceful figure swayed under about eighty loaves of bread, which she carried on a tray on her head. "Thabitah," said I, "our stars did not prove in harmony. You have married another man, and I have been joined in wedlock to an American lady. But for old love's sake permit me to take your picture, just as you are, with this American camera." With a genial smile, Thabitah stood in front of the awfully mysterious machine, and thus enabled me to secure her image and carry it away to the strange country beyond the seas.

At the invitation of our old parish priest we attended mass in the church of my earlier years. Contrary to the rules, two chairs were placed for us near the reader's desk, where I used to stand during mass before I left the Church of

my fathers. There I gazed again at the old Miz-
peh, — altar of sacrifice, — the robed priest,
the pictures of saints, the candlesticks, and the
worshiping congregation. The priest sent us
two pieces of the *korban* — consecrated bread
— with which distinguished members of the
congregation are favored during mass, and
which is the symbolic remnant of the sacred
feast which was eaten at religious gatherings in
bygone days. That sense of reverence which I
have never failed to experience in a house of
worship of whatever faith, invested the hour
with solemnity. Nevertheless, what I had become in the New World could not be easily
reconciled to what I had been in the Old World.
The service awakened in me old feelings and
sentiments, but they were such feelings and
sentiments as one experiences while turning
over the pages of an old picture-book with
which one had been familiar in childhood.

As I looked at the worshipers before me gazing reverently at those material objects, made
sacred to them by long associations, I said to

THABITAH

myself, Suppose that all these objects were taken away from these persons, would they still know what their religion was? To the remote ancestors of these men, Jesus spoke in simple, fluid, living parables. Those parables have become hardened into material objects in the ancient ecclesiastical communions, and into rigid creeds at the hands of more modern theologians. Christ recognized neither of these forms. There is no greater warrant in his Gospel for an inflexible creed than for this lavish spectacle. Let those who find religious inspiration in such forms have them. For my part, I prefer that Christianity which was preached on the Mount, by the seaside, at Jacob's Well, and in the upper room on Mount Zion — the Christianity of the open air and the open mind.

The governmental, religious, and social institutions of the land of my birth seemed to me to be in distressing harmony with one another, and turned my gaze with a profounder sense of appreciation toward forward-looking America, the land of light, liberty, and active hopefulness.

I felt, as never before, that as an American citizen my religion must be as free, as progressive, and as hopeful as the genius of my adopted country.

While on that voyage and during a short stay in Naples and in England, whenever I found myself in the company of an enlightened person, whether preacher or layman, I took the opportunity to discuss with that person the "present state of the religious world." Of the clerical orders, I conversed with Catholics, Anglicans, Congregationalists, and Unitarians. What was pleasantly surprising to me in all such conversations was the fact that almost every person with whom I discussed the momentous question of religion impressed me with the idea that discontent with many of the old statements of religion, and a desire for new and more enlightened ones, was very strong among many men in all communions. By all this I was much encouraged and confirmed in my belief that in my limited sphere I was facing the light of a new and happier day.

AT THE TEMPLE GATE

But when, upon returning to America, I made my views more fully known in my Michigan parish, I was met with more determined opposition. As usually happens in such cases, a very lively local theological controversy of a few months' duration, which in all probability would not have assumed such significance in a larger center of population, agitated and entertained the community. Of the many amusing incidents which occurred during that controversy, the following are samples.

After hearing one of my liberal sermons, an elderly gentleman of impenetrable conservatism, was asked what he thought of the discourse. "Well, sir," was his prompt and decisive answer, "it is the surest way to hell that I know of."

A good Methodist, an old man of saintly purity, called on me one day to express his regrets at my departure from "sound doctrine." At my invitation, the good man dined with us. In the course of our conversation, he assured me that I was in danger of eternal damnation because, in the sight of God, I was no better than a drunkard. "But," I asked, "Brother G., if the matter were left to you, would you throw me into such a lake of fire and brimstone as you believe hell to be?" "Of course not. I would n't do it." "Don't you think, Brother G., that God is as sensible and as good as you are?" With no little perplexity Mr. G. said, "He must be much better than I am. He is — well — God works in mysterious ways!"

Fourteen years have elapsed since I fought the decisive battle of my religious freedom and followed definitely the open road of the religion of the spirit. Of these years, after leaving Morenci and previous to my settlement in Boston, I spent two years in Mount Pleasant, Michigan, and nine of joyous ministerial activities in the youthful and progressive city of Toledo, Ohio. During these years, having been deprived of a regular college course, I have followed the path of my destiny in the world, not as a *learned*, but as a *learning*, man. I have always sought to conserve the truths of the past. I have listened eagerly to the voices of scientists, philosophers, sociologists, and theologians. So far as my time and ability have permitted, I have acquainted myself with "Evolution," the "New Psychology," the "Higher Criticism," "Social Religion," and other fields of modern research. My contact with such men and systems of thought has been to me like the contact of the "men of Athens" with Paul on Mars hill: they all say to me, "The God whom you ignorantly worship, Him declare we unto you."

Every step forward confirms me in my belief that God's judgments are those of a loving Father, that Christ's mission is to awaken all men to their divine sonship, that religion is life, and salvation spiritual self-fulfillment. And I find it neither possible nor just to think of myself as the pupil and beneficiary of any one church or denomination to the exclusion of all others. I am the grateful child of the whole Church of Christ, regardless of sect and creed.

But I am particularly indebted to those communions whose activities have influenced my life in a more direct way.

To my Mother Church, the Greek Orthodox, I am indebted for the earliest spiritual inspiration which flowed into my life in the name of Christ. Notwithstanding the pagan traits which still cling to her, that ancient church fixed my eyes in childhood and youth upon the cross of Christ as symbol of the soul's victory over sin and death.

To the missionary zeal of the great Presbyterian denomination, and to its firmness in the Christian faith as it is known to its members, I am indebted for my first lessons in the religion of an open Bible, and of individual conviction. It was in that Presbyterian school on the western slopes of my native Lebanon that I first learned to think of Christianity as a personal and not a corporate religion.

To the Methodist Episcopal Church of America I owe the profoundest sense of spiritual fervor. In my lonely days of poverty and struggle, when America was yet a strange land to me, the brotherly spirit and friendly touch of Methodism did more than any other one church influence to renew my strength and steady my faltering steps. And I trust that no modern revolutions, either in science or theology, will ever lead that communion to lose its noble and apostolic spirit of friendliness.

To the Congregational Church, both Trinitarian and Unitarian, I owe the largest measure of theological freedom and the highest level of spiritual thought I have yet attained. And I believe it is fitting, at the close of this story of my religious evolution and in connection with the preceding paragraph, for me to add the following.

About seventy-two years ago, when the Trinitarian-Unitarian controversy was going on among the Congregational churches of New England, the noted scholar, patriot, and preacher, the Reverend James Freeman Clarke, D.D., organized a church in the city of Boston. In order to save that church from the theological contentions of the period, he would have for it no doctrinal conditions of membership, but founded it on the simple basis of spiritual discipleship to Jesus Christ, with the sole object of coöperation in the study and practice of Christianity; and called it "The Church of the Disciples." Although the members of this Church have come from among the "liberals," its pulpit has never given itself to acrimonious controversial preaching. The deep spiritual insight of its founder led him to realize that the controversy between "liberals" and "orthodox" dealt largely with the non-essentials of Christianity, and that the essentials were common to both factions. Time has proved his wisdom. It is now my privilege to serve this free church whose altar bears this inscription: "In the freedom of the Truth, and in the spirit of Jesus Christ, we unite for the worship of God and the service of man." It was indeed most gratifying to me that at the service of my installation as minister of this church both wings of Congregationalism were represented.

CHURCH OF THE DISCIPLES, BOSTON, MASSACHUSETTS

Now, do you wish to know what riches I have gathered in the New World? I will tell you. These are my riches, which neither moth nor rust can corrupt. I have traveled from the primitive social life of a Syrian village to a great city which embodies the noblest traditions of the most enlightened country in the world. I have come from the bondage of Turkish rule to the priceless heritage of American citizenship. Though one of the least of her loyal citizens, I am rich in the sense that I am helping in my small way to solve America's great problems and to realize her wondrous possibilities. In this great country I have been taught to believe in and to labor for an enlightened and coöperative individualism, universal peace, free churches, and free schools. I have journeyed from the religion of "authority for truth" to the religion of "truth for authority" — a religion which teaches me the fatherhood of God, the brotherhood of man and the friendliness of the universe, and makes me heir to all the prayers, songs, and sermons of the ages. I am privileged to occupy the office of a minister of religion — the holiest vocation in the possession of man. I enjoy the blessings of a happy home, and daily bread comes to me and mine as regularly as it came to Elijah when he was being fed by the ravens. In all these things I am unspeakably rich; my dividends are large and constant and the source of my blessings seems inexhaustible. Last but not least of my spiritual companions is my "Aim of Life," which I rejoice to hear the children and young people in my Sunday School repeat together at their meetings: —

> Our aim is to conquer
> Ignorance by Knowledge,
> Sin by Righteousness,
> Discord by Harmony,
> Hatred by Love.

THE END

APPENDIX

APPENDIX

In compliance with the many requests which came to me while this autobiography was being published in the "Atlantic Monthly," I will state the essential agreements and differences between the Greek and Roman, or the Eastern and Western, Churches, in the language of a noted church historian: [1] —

"Both Churches own the Nicene Creed (with the exception of the *Filioque*), and all the doctrinal decrees of the seven œcumenical synods from A.D. 325 to 787, including the worship of images. They agree, moreover, in most of the post-œcumenical or mediæval doctrines, namely: the authority of ecclesiastical tradition as a joint rule of faith with the holy Scriptures; the worship[2] of the Virgin Mary, of the

[1] With slight abbreviation, from Philip Schaff's *History of the Christian Church*, vol. IV, pp. 306–08.

[2] Both the Greek and Roman communions assert that they do not *worship*, but *adore* the Virgin Mary and the saints.

saints, their pictures (not statues), and relics; justification by faith and good works, as joint conditions; the merits of good works, especially voluntary celibacy and poverty; the seven sacraments or mysteries (with minor differences as to confirmation, and extreme unction or chrisma); baptismal regeneration and the necessity of water-baptism for salvation; transubstantiation and the consequent adoration of the sacramental elements; the sacrifice of the mass for the living and the dead, and prayers for the dead; priestly absolution by divine authority; three orders of the ministry, and the necessity of an episcopal hierarchy up to the patriarchal dignity; and a vast number of religious rites and ceremonies.

"In the doctrine of purgatory, the Greek Church is less explicit, yet agrees with the Roman in assuming a middle state of purification. The dogma of transubstantiation, too, is not so clearly formulated in the Greek Creed as in the Roman. The Greek Church has never prohibited the popular use of the Holy Scriptures, but her traditions are as strong a barrier against the exercise of private judgment as those of Rome.

"The dissensus of the two Churches covers the following points:—

"1. The procession of the Holy Spirit: the East teaching the single procession from the Father *only;* the West (since Augustine), the double procession from the Father *and the Son* (*Filioque*).

"2. The universal authority and infallibility of the Pope, which is asserted by the Roman, is denied by the Greek Church. The former is a papal monarchy; the latter a patriarchal oligarchy.

"3. The immaculate conception of the Virgin Mary, proclaimed as a dogma by the Pope in 1854; disowned by the East.

"4. The marriage of the lower clergy, allowed by the Eastern, forbidden by the Roman Church (yet conceded by the Pope to the United Greeks).

"5. The withdrawal of the cup from the

laity. In the Greek Church the laymen receive the consecrated bread dipped in the wine and administered with a golden spoon.

"6. A number of minor ceremonies peculiar to the Eastern Church, such as trine immersion in baptism, the use of leavened bread in the Eucharist, infant-communion, the repetition of the holy unction in sickness."

The Riverside Press

CAMBRIDGE . MASSACHUSETTS

U . S . A